A Story of Love, Faith and Loot by

Facebook Friend

notionpress
.com

A Story of Love, Faith and Loot by

Facebook Friend

Anindita

notionpress.com

Notion Press

Old No. 38, New No. 6
McNichols Road, Chetpet
Chennai - 600 031

First Published by Notion Press 2016

ISBN 978-93-5206-935-4

Preface

This is a story of love, faith and loot by a Facebook friend. I want to share my experiences with social networking site users. I know that anyone who reads my story will laugh at me and will mark me as the most stupid woman in the country, and nobody will believe that I could not find an escape route from my so-called friend, alias cybercriminal. Nowadays, everybody is addicted to social networking sites, but how many of us know that through this medium cybercriminals plan schemes to trap people, to loot them? In earlier days, robbers used to rob the rich people going to their home, but nowadays, through advancement in technology, cybercriminals rob people by sitting in safe and distant places, leaving behind hardly any clue as to how they operate. Our ignorance about the modus operandi of these criminals and sometimes our greed also drag us into this pitfall, and smart criminals rob us mercilessly. For me, it was a story of friendship, a very new way of passing my lonely time with far-off friends and a window to look around the world, which turned into a gateway for cybercrime. I lost my lifetime savings; from a wealthy woman I became poor within a span of three months. It may happen to any other person. Believe me or not, every day many complaints are being lodged at the Cybercrime Police Stations across the country regarding various crimes that have their origins through Facebook, and the Police Departments do not have any magic wand to solve these crimes. Cybercrime Law 2000 and the subsequent amendment in 2008 are there to guide the police department on how to handle a complaint lodged in the field of cybercrime. But cybercriminals are extremely intelligent and invent various techniques to trap people unaware of their existence. However, if my story helps even a single person from being looted by cybercriminals, my effort to write my own story, with a lot of pain, will be remunerated.

Dedicated to FACEBOOK

Chapter One

Day One

It was a midsummer sultry night. This was only April, but the temperature was around 100° F; it was hot and humid, almost unbearable. I was alone at home, and could not concentrate on anything, reading, listening to music or watching TV, nothing could give me any pleasure. I opened my laptop and logged on to Facebook, and glanced through the posting of friends; some were good to give likes, but again that's a very boring thing. I was about to close FB when I noticed a friend request. I clicked on that and was amazed to see that someone named Jack Smith had sent me a friend request. I clicked on to his profile and saw he was a graduate from London School of Economics, and had done engineering as well. Originally, his family was from Blitz City of South America, but presently they were living in London, and he was working with a construction company as Chief Engineer at Liverpool. I was impressed by his graduation status, my dream university, London School of Economics; if someone from there wants to be my friend how could I not accept it! I confirmed his friend request.

Almost instantly, I received a "Thank u" message in a private chat window. I was excited, no doubt, as it would be a very new way of passing my lonely time. So, we started chatting.

Anindita: Hi, you are Jack Smith from London School of Economics, right?

Jack: Yes dear.

Anindita: Why did you send me a friend request?

Jack: I was in search of an old friend named Anna, and in the list your name appeared, and I was just smitten by your smiling face; I liked your profile, I must say, I am impressed. Will you accept me as your lifelong friend?

Anindita: I already accepted your friendship, did not I? You know, I liked your profile also, someone from London School of Economics, my dream institute, I love the subject Economics so much. I wish I could have studied there. You are so lucky. Tell me more about the institute. How were your experiences over there?

Jack: It was good. It was such a vast subject, with no end to its information. But I like engineering more. Are you single?

Anindita: No, but why? If I am not single would you not like to chat with me?

Jack: No, not that. I would love to chat. What do you do?

Anindita: Nothing special to be mentioned at present, but I have a specific plan to do some social work in future. I am on sabbatical to plan out my future course of actions. What do you do?

Jack: I am an engineer, working with a company on contract basis.

Anindita: After B. Sc from London School of Economics, did you study Engineering?

Jack: Yes dear.

Anindita: Great! Presently, in what nature of job are you engaged with?

Jack: It's a project at Liverpool, we are setting up a gas line under the Red Sea. It's a huge project.

Anindita: Oh! What a wonderful thing to do! How is the weather there? It's very hot and humid in our country, unbearable.

Jack: It's very pleasant here.

Anindita: I wish I could be there.

Jack: If you want to relocate, I will be most happy. I welcome you to my life, you are so beautiful!

Anindita: Hey, don't flirt with me. I am not beautiful, may be a little graceful, but I may be senior to you. Moreover, I love my country and am happily settled with a loving family.

Jack: Age is a number dear. If you are a few years older to me, it does not matter at all; we could be good friends or may be very close friends as well.

Anindita: Jack, you seem to be quite diplomatic in your conversation. What is your position in the company?

Jack: I am Chief Engineer heading a group of twenty-four engineers.

Anindita: That's quite a responsible job, I suppose.

Jack: Yes dear, it's tough. Our site is in a remote place and I stay in a lodge at Liverpool.

Anindita: How far is your workplace from the lodge?

Jack: It's a one-hour journey by jeep. My days are very hectic.

Anindita: I feel sorry for that. Why did you take such an assignment? You must be having a family?

Jack: I am a wealthy man but my wife died last year in a car accident.

Anindita: Oh! Very sorry to know that. Who are there in your family?

Jack: I have a daughter of eight years, living with my mother in London; my father was in the British Army and passed away when I was fifteen years old. My mother was a doctor and it was she who brought me up. Now she is old and stays at home; there are two helping nannies who look after them.

Anindita: I have heard that finding help for household work in London is very expensive.

Jack: Yes dear, I am a rich man, so no problem as such. How do you manage your household work?

Anindita: In India, labor is very cheap you know. So, I have the luxury of having two maids for my daily work.

Jack: Good. I love your status and wish you would not take any stress in life. I would love to see you someday.

Anindita: You are most welcome to India. Nice talking to you. We will chat some other day. It's time to go to bed.

Jack: Ok, my beautiful lady. Hope you will be available tomorrow also; I would love to chat with you. Bye.

We closed our chat window and I was quite happy to have a friend of such high stature.

DAY TWO

Next day after supper, I was eagerly waiting for the clock to strike eleven, so that I could find Jack in FB. At around 11.30 p.m, I opened the chat window to see if Jack was available. Yes, there he was. It may be around 6 p.m according to London time. I clicked on his window,

"Are you there honey?" Jack posted.

Anindita: Hey, are you addressing me as honey? I don't mean to be your honey dear. Address me by my name. By the way, your name is Jack or James? In your profile it was mentioned as Jack Smith, but now in your chat window it's showing James!

Jack: My friends lovingly call me as James sometimes.

Anindita: Okay. James Smith was a famous economist, you must be knowing that. Do you know the meaning of my name?, A person without any bad reputation. I love my name and will be happy if you please address me by my name only.

Jack: It's my feeling for you; since last night I have been thinking about you and have thanked God so many times for giving me a chance to be your friend.

Anindita: You seem to be very fast in your decision. Do you believe in God?

Jack: Oh! Very much. Only because of God's grace, I have come to the level where I am at present.

Anindita: Really? Do you mean to say that you did not have to rely on effort, quality and opportunity to come this far?

Jack: Yes honey, God is there always with me.

Anindita: So, you are a God-fearing person. Okay, let us talk about something else. Which discipline did you like most during your study time? Economics or Engineering?

Jack: Economics is such a vast subject! Right now Engineering is my love.

Anindita: Okay. I presume you do not have time to read also. You know, although I am in service, but my first love is Fine Arts; if I were given a chance, I would like to be a writer or singer, or may be a painter even, I love these disciplines.

Jack: If you write, I can help you in publishing your book from London.

Anindita: Really? I wish I could start now. But, I enjoy my music lessons also.

Jack: Do you sing? Wonderful. You have versatile qualities.

Anindita: No dear, I am always a learner. But, what about you? How do you spend your leisure time? You must have a liking for sports, what sports do you like most?

Jack: If I get time I watch wrestling.

Anindita: My! What a bad taste. Don't you like cricket, football or tennis?

Jack: Yes, I watch Football Premier Leagues.

Anindita: Jack, you know I am so excited about the coming World Cup Football Championship. We, Bengalis, passionately love cricket and football, both.

Jack: Really? What else do you like? What worldly things do you love?

Anindita: I love good books, books and only books, and association of wise and kind-hearted people, which is not easily available, I just can't mix up with common folk.

Jack: That's why you are so special to me.

Anindita: Don't flatter me. You hardly know me.

Jack: Honey tell me more about you, I would love to know.

Anindita: You know, I am fortunate and proud to be a Bengali. We have a great cultural heritage; we are regarded as the most cultured people in India. Have you heard about our great poet Rabindranath Tagore or the famous Economist Amartya Sen. Both are Noble Laureates.

Jack: Really? But I do not know much about them.

Anindita: I feel sorry for those who do not have strong cultural heritage, it's such a strength.

Jack: Honey, may I request you one thing. To strengthen our bonding, may I send you a present.

Anindita: What, present! I don't accept presents from strangers.

Jack: Honey, why do you call me a stranger! Am I not your friend yet?

Anindita: Yes virtual friend, but I hardly know you. I do not like to take anything from you.

Jack: Honey, you are my long-cherished friend. We were destined to know each other. I am surly going to meet you whenever my contract with this company is over by the end of July.

Anindita: Okay, you are most welcome in India. But, you may be disappointed with the meeting. We may not like each other at all if we meet. Better not to take the risk!

Jack: Why are you telling so? I know I will be very happy to meet you. Presently, will you please make me happy by accepting a humble gift from me?

Anindita: Jack, why do you want to spoil this relationship by this giving gifts, I really don't need anything.

Jack: Honey, its Easter time, and we send gifts to relatives, friends and all close relations. Now you are my friend, I will be so happy to send you gifts.

Anindita: When you will come to meet me, I will accept a gift from you for sure. Not now. Okay, bye for tonight. It's past midnight, high time to go to bed.

Jack: Ok, my sweet lady. Have good bed rest. Bye.

We closed our chat windows that night. But, I must admit that I loved to chat with him. He seemed to be a really good person.

DAY THREE

Next night, as usual, I opened Facebook at around 11.30 pm and found another friend request from someone named Mark Bright from London. I opened his profile and found that he was from Lee University, and was engaged in business. I was not impressed and was about to decline the request, but after a second thought, just to compare the statuses of both the people from London, I accepted that request also.

There was no instant reply, but Jack Smith was online.

Anindita: Hi, Jack, how are you?

Jack: Oh honey! I was missing you. How are you? What you are doing now?

Anindita: Chatting with you no doubt. So how was your day?

Jack: Very hectic dear. What did you do during the day?

Anindita: I had my music class to attend.

Jack: Really? I would love to listen to your music when I come to India to meet you. But you will have to sing an English song. I will record it so that I can hear it when I am back in London.

Anindita: You are dreaming too much and really moving very fast.

Jack: Why do you say so? You don't know what you mean to me now. You are my world.

Anindita: I can't be your world, okay? You have a lovely daughter, what's her name?

Jack: Jenny. I will send you some of our pictures.

Anindita: Yes do send, I love children.

Jack: You have a loving heart, but not kind enough to listen to my request.

Anindita: What request?

Jack: Please tell me what would you like to receive from me as presents?

Anindita: Nothing, I don't require anything. You know I have a foundation in my parents' name through which I try to help meritorious girl students pursue their studies. If you want, you may contribute something for them.

Jack: Oh sure, I would love to help you. But I would again be very happy if you accept something from me as a token of friendship.

Anindita: You have money, then why don't you buy valuable paintings or the diary of Leonardo da Vince from Bill Gates. Spend money on good things, not on me. I don't want to exploit a multimillionaire friend.

Jack: Honey, you make me sad. You know, I had a friend on Facebook with whom I used to chat every day and we were very close. One day, she asked me to help her with her medical expenses for her treatment; I sent her forty-five thousand GBP. But thereafter, she blocked me. I was so depressed for a long time.

Anindita: No wonder people cheat you. Within two days, you want to send me gifts! But I really don't need anything.

Jack: Honey, if you send me even flowers, I will accept it and be very happy.

Anindita: Okay, you send me flowers then, I will be happy.

Jack: Honey, you don't believe me, but you mean so much to me.

You are in my life now. I miss you all the time.

Anindita: You Europeans are very fast in making and breaking a relationship, I know that.

Jack: Honey, you don't believe me, I feel sad. But you will feel my love very soon. Please accept something from me, I will be happy.

Anindita: Sorry, I can't make you happy. You are my virtual friend, be happy with that. You find someone suitable for your age and get married, I will send you good presents, okay?

Jack: Honey, stop it. I don't want anybody else.

Anindita: I think you are tired and hungry too. Better call it a day. Bye.

Jack: Honey, just know I love you so much. There has to be a token of my love for you, please agree with that and let me know what I should send for you. Would you like to have, a laptop dear? It's very cheap here.

Anindita: No I have my laptop, and don't want another.

Jack: Then what else you would like dear?

Anindita: Nothing but your friendship.

Jack: We will remain friends forever, but any material thing may enhance our bonding.

Anindita: Okay, if you so insist, send me a simple wristwatch for daily use.

Jack: Thank you honey, I will buy it today itself and show it to you first.

Anindita: Don't you want to know, of all things why did I ask you to send a wristwatch? I will wear it as a friendship band from a far-off friend. Will it not be very romantic?

Jack: Oh dear, I am honored! I love you so much.

Anindita: Okay, it's getting too late, I will be logging off now. Good night!

Jack: Good night dear, have sweet dreams. I will miss you.

I must confess that I was enjoying the conversations with Jack. He was educated, rich and having a good position at work; moreover, his smiling face had something that I liked most; I was impressed and was eagerly waiting to chat with him. My lonely nights had some excitement no doubt.

I was thinking about Jack. To gather more impression about the city he was from and about Liverpool, where he was currently working, I opened Wikipedia. I was amazed to know that Blitze city was such a small place, only seven lakh+ inhabitants. Compared to our country, it was only a tiny place. Liverpool, a port city so sparsely populated, from the photo posted in Wiki, even appeared to be a well-maintained city on par with European standards. I remembered that Liverpool was very famous for its Premier League Football team. So, Jack must be having a nice stay over there. I was imagining so many things about the place and eagerly waiting to share my acquired knowledge and to know many more things from Jack. I wished I could travel to those places. Liverpool, being beside the Red Sea, must be a place worth seeing. I was really eager to talk to Jack about all these and was waiting for the next night to come when we would open our chat window.

DAY FOUR

It was Bengali New Year day. I was attending a social gathering in our housing complex. Jack called me in my cell phone and wished me happy Bengali New Year. I was so happy hearing his voice. It was not very British; rather to some extent, it had an American accent. I thanked him for his New Year wishes and he requested me to open my FB window to see the Easter gifts he had bought for me.

I rushed back to my house and opened my FB window. My! He had posted a picture of a diamond-studded Rolex wristwatch that he was holding in his palm, and a diamond necklace and bangles.

I was so annoyed to see all these expensive things and instantly I wrote back, "I will not accept these gifts, as I only wanted a simple wristwatch, not Rolex, and secondly I don't like jewelry. Whatever little I have, I hardly use those."

"Honey," Jack wrote back, "Why wouldn't you accept, it's nothing expensive, half of my riches is yours. You don't believe me now I know, but when we will meet, you will realize how much I love you. I will be so happy if you put on those jewelries when I visit India."

Anindita: Jack, excuse me, you are making me sick. I can't accept all these things just like that.

Jack: Honey, please, please try to understand. It's my feelings, you need not reciprocate, but at least honor my love.

Anindita: What love! I don't believe love can happen so quickly.

Jack: Honey, it can happen, you must be knowing that people fall in love at first sight.

Anindita: Jack, I don't want to argue with you on this matter but just try to understand. How would I justify to my husband as to why somebody has sent me such expensive gifts?

Jack: Honey, can't a friend send gifts to a friend?

Anindita: Jack, I am really fed up; I have to lie to my husband or I have to take delivery of the same outside my house, it will be very embarrassing for me.

Jack: Honey, I will be so happy. Please give me your address.

Anindita: Jack, your happiness might make me unhappy forever. I am satisfied with my present standing and status in life. I don't want to spoil that. I am not the person for your life, you find someone of your status please.

Jack: Honey, I don't demand anything from you but I do not want any other person in my life. Whichever way you will be there, I will be happy. But, please give me your address.

Day Five

At around 11.30 p.m, I opened my chat window and saw a posting from Jack, a few minutes back saying,

"Are you there honey? I miss you."

I was happy to know that Jack is missing me.

Anindita: Hi, so you are back from site. What's the time over there, around 6 p.m?

Jack: Yeah, I can't wait any longer to talk to you. So, came back early and just logged in to find you.

Anindita: How was your day?

Jack: Hectic honey. How are you?

Anindita: Why is it hectic always? Being Chief Engineer, you are not supposed to do things by yourself.

Jack: Honey, it's not so easy. I am supposed to be responsible for all and everything.

Anindita: Are you! Anyway every job has its own hazards. Let us talk on something else. When will you have your dinner?

Jack: I will have dinner after a few minutes, and take a shower thereafter. I am hungry but would like to talk to you for sometime.

Anindita: You know, we Indians take shower first and then take meal, just the opposite. We will find so many differences in culture, habits, likes and dislikes.

Jack: Those do not matter when you really love someone.

Anindita: I do not believe that absolute love can happen at this age.

Jack: Yes honey, it can happen, at least from my side. I am so sure about it.

Anindita: Nice to hear all these wonderful words! I am sorry I am detaining you. Aren't you getting late for supper? Please go ahead. I would not mind to log off.

Jack: No honey, please chat for sometime. I love to chat with you.

Anindita: You know, I was going through Wiki and read all about Easter festival, Blitz city and Liverpool even. Now I can imagine a little about you people.

Jack: Really? Tell me something about your country dear.

Anindita: Our country is overcrowded. Everywhere you will find people and people only. Majority of our people are poor, they hardly get two square meals. But, we have enough natural resources, rich cultural heritage and a very strong philosophical outlook towards life. You may not feel it from outside.

Jack: Honey, I could understand it from your words. I will know it more when we will be together.

Anindita: How? What do you mean by that!

Jack: I will come to India to see you, as soon as my contract with the company is over. I miss you so much.

Anindita: Jack, don't be funny, okay? Why should you miss me! You hardly know me. You should miss your late wife.

Jack: I miss her too but now you are in my life and I miss you very much.

Jack, we better log off tonight, it's time for your dinner.

Ok honey. Tomorrow we will chat again. Just know, I love you so much.

We logged off. But, Mark Bright was online. I wanted to chat with him just to compare the two people from the same city. So, I opened the chat window of Mark Bright.

Anindita: Hi Mark Bright, how are you?

Mark: Hi dear, how are you? In what profession you are engaged now? What do you do nowadays?

Anindita: Nothing as such, just enjoying life.

Mark: Oh really, but I wish you could be my business partner in India. I wanted to invest in real estate in India. Will you join me?

Anindita: Sorry, I don't have any interest in real estate business nor am I interested in making money. At best, I can name big real estate business icons in India where you may invest money.

Mark: If you help me, I shall remunerate you.

Anindita: No thank you, I don't want to be related to your business in any way.

Mark: I heard an Indian woman is very good and could be a loving and trusting wife. I am in search of a good life partner; I have been cheated by someone, so very scared of my own clan.

Anindita: Sorry to know that, but who told you about Indian woman?

Mark: A friend of mine.

Anindita: Did not he tell you that Indians are very conservative in their outlook and not at all adventurous about life?

Mark: But you are not that type; if you were not married, I would have proposed to you.

Anindita: Really? And you thing I would have jumped to your proposal! You people are very funny.

Mark: Why? I am rich and capable of taking responsibilities.

Anindita: Okay, that does not qualify you as a groom, understand? There is a big cultural gap between Europe and India; it's not compatible at all; anyway, why don't you find someone from your own communities.

Mark: No, I don't like my community woman; they are self-centered and treacherous.

Anindita: I don't believe that all are bad. Keep an open eye; you may be lucky someday.

Mark: I am very choosy no doubt. How is your love life?

Anindita: I enjoy my life in all respects; however, I am getting late, better call it a day. By the way, are you English?

Mark: No, I am Irish, originally we were in Ireland.

Anindita: Nice to know you. We may chat some other day, bye.

Mark: Ok bye. Good night.

We closed the chat windows but I was amazed to see that these guys are all in search of life partners through FB. How funny? Do they really mean it or was there some other purpose, I doubt. But somehow, I was not impressed by Mark Bright; he appeared to be very skeptic, too much business minded! But, I decided to continue chatting with him also just to compare my very own feelings for these two different people with different backgrounds from the city of London. None of them were English, that was good. I did not want to be friendly with those who ruled our country for 200 years. However, I had found a nice way to pass my lonely time with these far-off friends. That's not bad, I told to myself, and went to sleep.

Day Six

It was Friday and I had to attend my music class, but it was a hot and humid day; I didn't feel like going out; putting on the AC also could not cool down the suffering; that year, summer was heating us badly. However, as I was thinking whether I should attend the class or not, Jack called me and said,

Honey, I have dispatched your gifts, it will reach you within two or three days.

"Don't you have any other work but to send gifts to FB friends! To how many friends did you send gifts this year?" I asked him jokingly.

Jack: Honey, why did you say so! I have no other friend but you.

Anindita: Okay, cool, you are supposed to be in your seashore site at this time, did not you go to work?

Jack: Yes honey, I will not be going there today. I have some office work. And dispatching the consignment was another agenda. What are you doing now honey?

Anindita: I will be changing to a saree to go to attend my music class. By the way, have you seen any saree-wearing woman?

Jack: No honey! How is it ?

Anindita: Okay, I will upload a picture of mine in saree, which is known as the most beautiful and graceful dress for a woman, you know.

Jack: I would love to see that.

Anindita: Hey, you were supposed to upload pictures of your daughter. When will you do that?

Jack: Ok, honey, I will upload it today itself along with the consignment dispatch slip.

Anindita: I shall see it at night, now I will be going to music class. Bye.

Jack: Bye honey!

At night, I opened my Facebook chat window and saw that Jack had posted a few pictures with his daughter. Jenny appeared to be a very charming kid of seven or eight years. I liked her, and in return, I also posted a few pictures of my family with my son, husband and a picture of mine wearing a saree, just to impress him.

It was too early for Jack to log on to chat window as it was only 4.30 pm at London time; he should be in office then. So, I left a note for him to be available for chat at twelve o'clock Indian time.

But I got a call from him as he was impatient to talk to me.

Jack: Honey, are you free now? If so, let us log on to chat window, I miss you terribly.

Anindita: Don't you have any work today or what?

Jack: I left office early.

Anindita: Okay, I have seen your pictures, its lovely. It seems you are very tall. What is your height? Not less than 6.2 inches, I suppose.

Jack: I am 6.4.

Anindita: Quite a giant size. My! You are taller than the American President Barak Obama and Raghuram Rajan, our RBI Governor! You know, I am a great admirer of these two personalities. But, I like your ever-smiling face, and your daughter too. Have you seen my family pictures?

Jack: Yes honey, you have a wonderful family. What's your son doing?

Anindita: He is a scholar, interested to do Ph.D., may be somewhere in USA, or Canada or Singapore.

Jack: Better to do it at Canada, best place.

Anindita: Why do you think so? If it is at Singapore it will be nearer to India. I would prefer that.

Jack: But Singapore is a small place; he will be bored and those Chinese people are self-centered. Their food habits are also awful.

Anindita: You are very fussy about food, it seems. Chinese food is famous all over world. We like it.

Jack: Casual dining with Chinese food is ok, but for long, it's not acceptable. I don't like it at all.

Anindita: What are your favorite dishes?

Jack: Fried Rice, chicken and salad.

Anindita: Sounds very Indian, stereotypical food. However, we have so many options on food, especially as Bengal is a very fertile land. We get a variety of vegetables and fishes.

Jack: Really? What are your favorite dishes, dear?

Anindita: It's simple! We mainly have rice, dal, some fried vegetables, fish curry and salad in our daily meal. And you know, we are so fond of sweets, I bet even you would like Bengali sweets.

Jack: Sure, whatever you will give me I would love that. Let me visit you first.

However, have you seen the consignment note?

Anindita: No, is there anything to see there?

Jack: Yes dear, hope you would not mind to pay the delivery charges. Although I have made arrangement for that also.

Anindita: What you are talking about, I do not get it.

Jack: The courier will charge from the receiver a few dollars, as delivery charge of the consignment. So, I have put some bills inside a bag, very secured and in a safe way in a pink bag, no one will find that. On receipt of the parcel, your charges will be adjusted. I have send you a family album also, you will like it.

Anindita: What! You have sent bills inside the parcel? Are you mad or what? Don't you know sending cash this way is illegal? They will scan the parcel and will detect the cash and the entire thing will be confiscated. I will be put in trouble.

Jack: No honey, don't panic, it will not be detected.

Anindita: You are talking like a fool. Anyway how much did you put in the bag?

Jack: Honey, please don't get angry, it's only one million GBP.

Anindita: Jack, why did you put so much cash in the parcel? Did I ask you for any amount? Anyway, I shall not accept the parcel, that's final. I will ask them to return it to the sender.

Jack: Honey, why are you reacting this way? You have a NGO and you have lots of plans to expand its activities you said, and money will be required to fulfill your dream, take it easy.

Anindita: No, I don't want so much of money, especially when you have send it in an illegal way. I made a great mistake by agreeing to accept gifts from you.

Jack: Honey, you are making me sad, trust me I love you and want to see you happy with your activities. There are so many pictures in your profile of the destitute orphan girl children you are serving, so I thought of only helping you.

Anindita: Without asking me how did you do that? I don't understand; I have to face a lot of trouble for it. But how did you get so much of cash?

Jack: My company has given me 1.5 million GBP last month. Out of that I send you one million only.

Anindita: Jack, I am very much worried now, you have put me in trouble. I don't like it at all. You have spoiled my happy mood, don't feel like talking anymore, better call it a day. Bye.

Jack: Bye honey, please, please don't misunderstand me. I just want to make you happy, just know I love you so much, half of my riches is yours.

We closed the chat window. I was very upset. That night I could not sleep properly, and I did not know what awaited me in the future. I cursed myself for letting Jack indulge in such things. Outside the temperature was too high and my mind also was restless, no one was there to consult on this issue as I could not tell my husband that someone in a far-off place loved me and was sending me valuable gifts, GBP for my NGO activities, etc. I decided to face it alone.

Day Seven

It was getting very hot day by day, and because of humidity, it was getting unbearable; moreover, my household help had taken leave for a few days, so I was undone. And the anxiety over the issue of the parcel had added to the injuries. I was in a dilemma now, should I accept it or should I return it. The money inside the parcel was going to be detected for sure and it was illegal, and my name would be related to that, which I did not like at all. What would I do? All these thoughts were bothering me so much! My husband was so busy with pre-election duties, he hardly stayed at home. I was alone all the time, it was so frustrating! This is the curse of a nuclear family life. Nowadays, social networking site gave a feeling of togetherness with friends but that also had some limitations; on the whole, tragedy of a lonely life was very frustrating. And because of that, Jack had hypnotized me, I just couldn't avoid him. His background, expression of love and care for me was something that I enjoyed but again I knew that it was a very unusual relationship that I was getting into. Throughout the day, I thought about him and waited for chatting at night. As usual, I had opened my FB chat window at night around 11.30 pm and saw that Mark Bright was available. Instantly, I received a message from him, "Hi Anna, how do you do?"

Anindita: I am fine, what are you up to at this time?

Mark: I was thinking about you.

Anindita: Really! Why ? Don't you have any other thing to do?

Mark: Anna, why can't you be my business partner? You know I have a plan to expand my business in India, you could be a great help for me. I shall pay you consultancy charge.

Anindita: Don't be funny! I told you I am a happily married woman, not interested in any sorts of play. Moreover, I told you earlier also that I am not interested in business.

Mark: Ok, at least you find a good Indian woman for me.

Anindita: Why should I? You find one yourself; I don't like this type of conversation. You seem to be quite high.

Mark: Ok, sorry if I hurt you in any way. I have a call to attend. Will talk some other time.

Anindita: Okay, bye.

I was happy to log off. I found this Mark Bright as too boring, but he was very straightforward, and that's a good quality.

Jack opened his window, "Hi honey, how are you doing? I was missing you."

Anindita: I did not miss you, but your action compelled me to think about you.

Jack: I am so happy that you were thinking about me!

Anindita: You made me unhappy and getting pleasure out of that!

Jack: Why are you telling so dear?

Anindita: I am worried about your gift parcel. I don't think that I should accept it.

Jack: Honey, don't say such a thing. You should know how much I love you.

Anindita: If your love gives me trouble, why should I accept it?

Jack: No trouble will be there, nothing will happen.

Anindita: Okay, at present there is no need to argue on the issue. Tell me, how was your day?

Jack: To much of pressure, I have a severe headache.

Anindita: Tomorrow is a holiday for you or not?

Jack: No honey, I have to go to the site. May be on Sunday even. My senior usually comes on the weekend to review the progress and to give instructions if he has any.

Anindita: Oh! I thought I will talk to you throughout the day and will know many more things about you. But it seems you don't have time for me.

Jack: Yes dear, I would love to talk but I have to go to the doctor tomorrow morning to get drugs.

Anindita: What! Drugs? I think you will be visiting doctors for medicine for your headache.

Jack: Yes dear, may I ask your permission to log off, I want to take rest.

Anindita: Oh sure. Take care. Don't skip your dinner, it is very bad for health. Bye.

I logged off his window. But, I was not happy at all because I had wanted to discuss with him all possibilities and consequences that might arise on receipt of the parcel he had sent to me, but couldn't. I was not enthusiastic about receiving it at all. The whole night I was worried and did not sleep soundly either. But how could I ignore the love and sweet gesture Jack was showing for me! His smiling face had something, which attracted me the most. I thought someday I would ask him to appear on Skype to see actually how he looked like. Since morning, I was looking at the watch and calculating the time at Liverpool as I had planned to greet him with a "Good morning" and then to discuss the issues.

But Jack was not available on Facebook chat window, so I left a message for him, "Good Morning Jack, how are you? Hope your headache subsided and you had a sound sleep last night. Actually, I wanted to talk to you but it seems you are preoccupied; however, we should chat at night, okay?" Thereafter, I was going through my profile and was checking postings of my other friends, liking a few and keeping an eye to see if Jack opened his chat window. Yes, there he was! I clicked his window and saw he had posted, "Hi honey, are you there? Missing you so much. Actually I am waiting for my driver to come, I have to visit a doctor first, my headache is so severe, could not sleep last night."

Anindita: I am very sorry to know your suffering. Do you get it often?

Jack: Not always, it's because of too much stress. I really have very hectic days.

Anindita: Okay, visit your doctor first, I will be waiting for you at night.

Jack: Ok honey, take care of yourself, my driver is waiting, please permit me to leave. I will miss you.

Anindita: Bye, take care.

I was happy that at least I could talk to him for a while. It was time for my lunch, so I closed the window. Midsummer days seemed to be unbearably longer when someone was waiting for the night to come, as I was doing, and longing to chat with Jack at night! The heat and the anxiety about the contents of the parcel were enough to make things from bad to worse. I was restless throughout the day. My waiting came to an end at 12.30 pm at night, Jack was calling me...

Jack: Honey, are you there? Are you there? Missing you.

Anindita: Yes, I am very much here online. So, on Sunday also you don't have much time to talk to me, very bad.

Jack: You know, the doctor took much time and again I had a few guests also. However, I was missing you throughout the day.

Anindita: Liar, you need not explain things to me; anyway, how is your health now?

Jack: Okay dear.

Anindita: What is your program for tonight?

Jack: Nothing special, if you were with me I could have enjoyed the night. But what do I do alone?

Anindita: Why don't you go to see your daughter and mother during the weekend, its only four hours journey by air as you said.

Jack: You know, I am not permitted to leave the station till the contract is over.

Anindita: My! Very bad contract then. Now come to the point. You made a mistake by putting bills inside the parcel, I am very worried about that. It will be detected and my name will be associated with that, I don't like it at all.

Jack: Honey, don't worry, it will not be detected.

Anindita: Don't talk like a fool. Your act was very childish. You know Jack, when a child does something wrong the mother scolds the child but later on forgives the misdeed and hugs the child. You have acted like a child but I don't know if I could ever forgive you.

Jack: I have not done anything wrong. I have sent you, my love, a few gifts, that's all. And I deserve a hug and kiss from you.

Anindita: You are getting very naughty day by day.

Jack: Honey, just know I love you. Sorry I have a call, please excuse me for sometime.

Anindita: Okay. It's quite late at night, I am logging off. Bye.

Jack: Bye honey. See you tomorrow.

Mark Bright was calling me saying, "Hi Anna, how are you?"

Anindita: Fine. I did not expect you at this time, don't you have Sunday night party?

Mark: Yes, I spend the evening in a pub with a few friends, and just now came back. Please be online, let me take a drink from the freezer.

Anindita: I hope you are not drunk, I heard Irish are hardcore drinkers. What drink did you take?

Mark: Wine. Do you drink?

Anindita: Usually no. Sometimes if there is any party to attend, I go for wine.

Mark: Good, you could be a nice friend of mine, I like you. I don't have much time to spend with woman but I have found you are different than the usual type and very interesting.

Anindita: Really? How did you come to this conclusion?

Mark: I can understand people from their conversation.

Anindita: You have immense self-confidence, I suppose. In one way that is good, but in another way it may mislead you also. Better keep an open mind to accept anything. Anyway, tell me what you did during the day.

Mark: I went for Easter shopping.

Anindita: What did you buy?

Mark: Some decorative things for the house, a few gifts for friends and relatives, but I missed to buy anything for you.

Anindita: Thank God. Why should you buy anything for me! You saved me.

Mark: Why are you telling so, I should have bought something for you also.

Anindita: It's enough that even though we are from so far-off a place, we are keeping in touch, chatting on various things courtesy another MarkJu, not Bright of course. This is the blessings of information technology.

Mark: Yes, it's a great feeling, to be so close to a woman from a far-off place.

Anindita: Hey, you seem to be getting high. Better log off tonight. Bye.

Mark: Ok. Bye my sweet friend.

We logged off.

I remember a joke on Irish people and their drinking habit.

"A Texan walked into a pub in Ireland and threw a challenge to the hardcore drinker, saying that if anyone of them can drink ten pints of Guinness back to back he will give USD $500 to the drinker. Nobody accepted the challenge; one person even left the pub. But after thirty minutes, the man came back and asked if the challenge was still open? The Texan said, yes and asked the bartender to line up ten pints of Guinness. The Irishman tears open all and drinks them back to back. Other pub patrons cheer and the Texan sits in amazement, hands over USD 500 immediately and asks the Irishman that when he knew that he could drink the whole lot why did he leave the pub for thirty minutes? The Irish replied, 'I went down to another pub to see if I could drink back to back as you asked.'"

So I thought my friend Mark also may have such a wonderful drinking habit; else, how could he spend the whole evening with friends in a pub and again take a drink while talking to me? I thought to be careful in future while chatting with him. I had heard that Irish were very stingy also. How come he had thought of buying something for me as Easter gift! What was so special about celebration of Easter day? Was it like our Durga Puja Festival? I remembered that the other day I had read something about the celebration from Wiki, but it was nothing comparable to our Durga Puja.

Day Eight

It was Monday, start of a new week. A lot of things were awaiting me as I knew that Jack's parcel would arrive any day and I had to decide about it, should I accept it or should I return it, especially when I knew that very unusual things were there along with it. I was very anxious no doubt. I did not want to be associated with any illegal activities; there might be ways in every country to channelize illegal things as legal but I did not support that, so I had to take a right decision in this regard. I was restless since morning. At around twelve thirty, I received a call in my cell phone from someone named John; he introduced himself as representative of Skypack Expressway Delivery Service and informed me that a parcel has arrived in my name at their New Delhi office and asked me if it had to be delivered to my home address. I was confused as he did not mention anything else regarding the contents of the parcel, so I thought that things might have escaped their notice; however, if they delivered it to my home address my husband would know about it, so I told him to deliver it to my bank. He agreed to that and asked the bank address, and told that he would let me know when the deliveryman would be there. I was relieved.

At night, I logged on Facebook chat window at the usual time when Jack was supposed to be available and saw him online.

Anindita: Hi Jack, are you there?

Jack: Yes honey, I was waiting for you. How are you honey?

Anindita: Not fine, it is too hot over here. Moreover, your parcel has arrived. I don't know where to take delivery of that without the notice of my husband?

Jack: Did they say anything about the contents?

Anindita: No, nothing. They even did not say anything about the delivery charges I am supposed to pay.

Jack: Don't worry about that honey. It will not be much. All the more, it will be squared off once you get those pounds.

Anindita: I am still not sure if I should accept it from you.

Jack: Why honey! You have so many philanthropic activities to carry on.

Anindita: Yes dear, you know I was planning to buy a flat in the city where I could offer lodging to poor but meritorious girls who come to the city for study purposes. Your money may be utilized for that purpose. In our country, girl children of poor families are deprived in so many ways! They don't get proper food, education or treatment. I wish to help those girls. I don't know how far I will be able to do, but your money will help me a lot no doubt.

Jack: It's your money now, honey.

Anindita: No, no, I will associate your name in that project, if I could make it to reality. I want to make something exclusively for girls. Don't you think that it will be a great way to utilize your money?

Jack: Yes dear, I would love to support you.

Anindita: Anyway, how is your health today? Headache gone I suppose.

Jack: Yes, I am better today.

Anindita: Okay, you may be hungry, take your dinner and shower and go to sleep.

Jack: Yes honey, you are so caring. I love you so much.

Anindita: Welcome. Good night. Bye.

Jack: Bye honey.

We logged off.

Day Nine

Next day at around 11 am, I received a call in my cell phone from John. He said, "Madam, there is a problem raised in delivering the parcel, as while scanning it, a huge sum was detected inside the parcel, which is an illegal way of transferring money from a foreign country."

How much money is there? I asked.

John: It's one million GBP Ma'am.

Anindita: How did you know the amount? Have you opened the parcel?

John: Yes Mam, on detection of money inside the parcel we had to open it.

Anindita: So, what you are going to do with the sum?

John: Madam, you have to pay some fees to legalize the money.

Anindita: What fees! It can't be legalized. The authorities will call it a case of money laundering. I don't want to be associated with this. Please return the parcel to the sender.

John: Madam, there are ways to legalize it; we can help you.

Anindita: No thanks, I don't want to go through that underground process. I will tell the sender. I am not going to accept it.

John: Ok madam, I have to convey your opinion to my head office and they will take the decision. But madam, you need not be so worried, think over it. It's a huge sum; if it is channelized and gets legal entity you will be benefitted.

Anindita: No way. Being a responsible citizen of the country, I am not going to take part in any illegal activities.

John: Ok madam. As you wish. He ended the call.

I was so annoyed and angry with Jack, as because of his foolish way of sending bills, it had invited a lot of queries from the authorities. I wanted to inform him of the development, but right then he would be in office and I had to wait till 11.30 pm at night. But Jack called me on my cell phone and said, "Honey, how are you? I am missing you."

Anindita: I am not well at all, you know Mr John called me and said they have found a huge sum in the parcel, and are asking me if they could help me to legalize it. But I asked him to return it to the sender, as I don't want to be associated with any illegal activities, which goes against the law of our country.

Jack: Is it so? I am very sorry to know it. What else did he say? Are they going to return it?

Anindita: He will convey my instruction to their Head Office and they will take the decision on how to return it.

Jack: Honey, I did not mean to give you any trouble. But if there is any way they can help you to legalize the sum, will you not agree to that?

Anindita: No, because I know there will be lot of formalities related to that and everywhere my name will be associated, which I don't want.

Jack: Ok honey, as you wish. I am really upset now.

Anindita: Why should you be upset. You will get back your money and other gifts also.

Jack: It was for you dear, I don't want to get it back.

Anindita: I don't want to be involved in any illegal activities, understand? No need to argue on the issue. Bye.

Jack: Bye honey.

I was annoyed and did not feel like opening the chat window at night. As I knew, he would go on convincing me not to return his gifts. But I had decided not to take it for sure.

DayTen

Next day at around 10.30 am Mr John called me again saying, "Madam, there is a problem my head office told me to return the gift articles but money can't be returned as

British Government will sue against the company if money is returned. It is not permitted by the law of the country."

I was furious and refused to be convinced with his argument. I told him that I couldn't help it and it was the problem of their company; they should find a way to handle it, I was not going to accept the illegal sum.

He again tried to convince me that their company will get Anti-money Laundering Certificate from appropriate authorities, and on payment of certain fees, it would be legalized.

I told them not to bother me anymore, as I was not going to accept it.

"But madam, the parcel arrived in your name, you just can't keep away; sooner or later government authorities will call you and question why you are not receiving this; it's a huge sum, they will trouble you if it is not legalized," he kept pestering.

I was helpless, and didn't know what to do. Either way, I was in trouble, and cursed Jack for putting me in such a situation.

John told me to remit INR 35000 to a bank account number that he had mentioned with Union Bank Dimapore, as fees for returning the gift articles in the parcel.

I thought that at least this would save me from the embarrassment of receiving those costly gifts. I agreed to remit the sum knowing fully well that Dimapore was a place where all sorts of illegal activities took place; may be that courier company used those routes also for their business purposes. So, I remitted the sum to get rid of the problem. But the NEFT bounced back to my account for reasons not known to me. I had no way but to wait for further communication from Mr John the next day. I was so confused and felt utterly helpless, whom would I consult! I couldn't share my problem with my husband and did not have any one else to consult. I was waiting to consult Jack during our night chat. As usual at around 12.30, at night, I opened the chat window and found that Jack was online.

Jack: Hi honey, are you there online? I am waiting for you for so long. Are you ok dear?

Anindita: Hey, I told you to address me by my name not this honey, it sounds very ridiculous to me.

Jack: Why do you say so? I love you so much, why should I not call you honey?

Anindita: I am in such a big problem because of you only. They asked me to pay INR 35000 as fees for returning those gifts. I sent it, but it has bounced back. I don't want to channelize illegal money to my name but the company will not return it as it will invite legal problem for them! Can you tell me what should I do? I am in a trap now.

Jack: Cool honey, cool. Nothing will happen to you. Tomorrow is Good Friday, their office will remain closed so they can't return the parcel, so the fee was returned to your account. But they will really help you to legalize the sum by receiving Anti-money Laundering Certificate from British Government on payment of minimum fees. Then everything will be set right.

Anindita: I don't understand that if receiver is not willing to accept the parcel why they can't return it to the sender? Am I in any way responsible for all these? You are nothing but a stranger to me. Why should I accept such a huge sum from you?

Jack: Honey you are hurting me, did not I tell you what you do mean to me? I assure, if you face any problem, I will be coming to India and handling it myself. You trust me, dear.

Anindita: I am still in dilemma. I know the Indian system and procedure better than you; if once my name is associated with any illegal activity, the government authority will make my life hell. Moreover, how do I account for those huge sums? So many problems are cropping in my mind.

Jack: Please keep aside your anxiety. I shall take care of everything. I will be coming to India by the end of July and help you in all respects, just trust me and smile please.

Anindita: Okay. It's too hot over here and you have taken away my peace of mind also. Let's hope for the best.

Jack: That's like a good girl.

Anindita: Hey, I am not a girl, I am woman.

Jack: Yes, my lovely woman, I love you so much, and wish you love me too.

Anindita: You must be having three consecutive holidays, Good Friday, Saturday, and Sunday. What do you do during holidays in that remote place?

Jack: No dear, we will have work.

Anindita: Is it? So sad. I thought we would talk for longer hours. Did you have your dinner?

Jack: No, not yet, I shall be having it; actually I enjoy chatting with you, so I never mind late supper.

Anindita: I am very sorry, you better log off and take your dinner, shower, etc. Be online tomorrow at night. I will let you know if any development has happened in between. Bye, good night. We logged off.

I was about to close FB, but Mark Bright was online,

Mark: Hi Anna, I was waiting for you, have lot of things to discuss with you.

Anindita: Is it? Tell me what you want to talk about. Hope you are in your senses, not high with your evening course of drinks..

Mark: Oh dear, I am fine. I am planning to invest in India soon, I told you. Actually, I will be visiting your country next month itself and meeting you.

Anindita: Are you serious about that?

Mark: Yes I am. I have done a huge project at Dubai successfully, so now I will do another in your country.

Anindita: What type of project are you after?

Mark: I want to purchase land and make a housing project.

Anindita: My! You will need a reputed consultant for that, have you found any? It won't be easy to do anything in India, you should know rules and regulations very well.

Mark: You could have been a help.

Anindita: No dear, I don't have any knowledge in this field, but my husband has.

Mark: Do you have own house or residential flat?

Anindita: We have our own house.

Mark: Ok, nice. Can you give me any first-hand information about the cost of building a four-storied residential house in India.

Anindita: It depends on the area. It will vary from place to place; cost of construction in a megacity like Mumbai or Delhi is not comparable to other megacities like Kolkata, or Chennai even. Land acquisition is a huge hassle in megacities in India.

Mark: I have money, so I think I will be able to do it.

Anindita: Sorry, as far as my knowledge goes, only money will not work. If you really want to invest in India, it will be wise to invest in big Real Estate Companies.

Mark: Ok thanks for your advice. Let me work out my plan, I will let you know later on. I have a call now, bye my sweet friend.

Anindita: Bye, good night.

I logged off. I wondered how he would do business in India. It seemed that he did not have much of knowledge about our country! Anyway, I was not very much interested in him, let him do whatever he liked. I enjoyed talking to Jack and not Mark Bright.

I envied these people; they are living in a nice country, and had a cool weather; it was so hot over here, I had put on the AC but I couldn't sleep. My mind was restless as I was anxious about the arrival of the gift parcel. How would I handle it? I was asking myself repeatedly.

Day Eleven

Next day I received a call from Mr John saying, "Madam open your E-mail and see our Head Office has arranged a Antiterrorist Fund Clearance Certificate in favor of you, now you need not bother about legality of your fund, we can easily deposit it to Reserve Bank of India for conversion and to complete related formalities."

Anindita: Okay. I shall open my E-mail and let you know my decision.

John: Thank you madam.

So I opened my E-mail and in Inbox I saw the certificate as,

CERT. NO: 703991/04

THE UNITED KINGDOM

ORIGINAL

ANTI-TERRORIST LAWS ENFORCEMENT AGENCY

A COMPLETE COMMITMENT TO TOTAL FIGHT AGAINST TERRORISM

IN COLLABORATION WITH FEDERAL MINISTRY OF JUSTICE HAGUE-NETHERLANDS.

Anti-Terrorist Fund Clearance Certificate

In exercise of the powers conferred on this agency by the provisions of Anti-Terrorism Security Decree No. 54 of 2002 and of all other powers enabling this agency in that regard.

Anindita

Whose payment particulars has been verified, is hereby certified free from Terrorism-affiliated and Money Laundering subject to the provisions of the Decree and any conditions laid down/any regulations made thereunder.

Given under by hand and the Authority of the President

Chairman, Anti-terrorist Commitee

It was a weird certificate, with no date, and only a number. How could I believe that it would serve the purpose! I called back John and expressed my doubt. He assured me that it would serve its purpose as he had handled a similar case earlier also; he told that Reserve Bank accepted this certificate based on the number and signature.

I just didn't know what to do. So I thought to leave a note to Jack in the chat window. I wrote, "Jack I am doubtful about the certificate issued by the Chairman, Antiterrorist Committee, whether it will be acceptable by our Reserve Bank of India, but Mr John told me that he has handled a similar case earlier also and there will be no problem henceforth. You have put me in trouble, I still do not want to accept your money as it has come in an illegal way. Who knows what will be the aftereffects of channelizing the sum, my name will appear in the books of the government. I am a peace-loving citizen of India, why should I be involved in such things. You please ask the courier service to send it back."

To my utter surprise, Jack replied back within a few seconds saying,

"Honey, I am in office now, about to leave for the site, thought to check my chat window and see if you are available. I was missing you. Last night I just thought about you, could not sleep as I realized your anxiety about receiving the parcel. Honey, believe me there is nothing to worry so much. They are quite capable to handle such things. May be you have to bear some charges, but once you receive the remittance, it will be squared off. So, no need to be worried at all."

Anindita: Jack, I wish to believe you but I know there will be lot of formalities in between, and I have to go through those, which will not be easy to handle alone. I can't share it with my husband even.

Jack: Yes honey, I am a man. I know how he will feel if you tell him all these, honey please do not involve him, ok?

Anindita: You are a very bad person, should be ashamed of telling such a thing.

Jack: Yes honey, I am badly in love, so don't want to see anybody in between. As it is, your husband is a lucky person for having such a wonderful wife in life. Honey my driver is waiting, I should be off now.

Anindita: Okay, bye. Hope to chat at night.

Jack: Sure honey. Bye.

I was elated no doubt; it was nice to hear such lovely words from a far-off friend, and though I had not met him yet, I had also started loving him. I wished that someday or other we would have a chance to enjoy each other's company. I loved Jack. I started planning to receive Jack when he would come to India to meet me and see my NGO activities. Where should I put him? In Taj Bengal or in ITC, Sonar or in Oberoy Grand? No not at Oberoy, as it was in the heart of city and a very crowded place. I would prefer ITC, Sonar; I had to see what would be his choice, after all I did not have any idea about the fancies of a rich man. Would he like to visit a few places in India? If he wanted, where should I take him? Darjeeling or Kashmir or Delhi, Rajasthan? I had to consult him before making any plans. He may not be knowing anything about those places so I had to tell him the specialty of each place. Oh my! I was really going too far, I scolded myself and started getting ready for my music class.

It was very hot that year. We used to hardly get the Northwestern monsoon, and temperature was rising every day. I wondered why we had to go for Lok Sabha election during the summer? They could have preponed it; our political leaders had their own agenda and were not bothered about the hardships faced by the general public. I had no interest in politics, but again I knew that since time immemorial, political leaders were the driving factors for the development of a country. We were the largest democratic country having freedom of speech and so many other rights, but standard of living of the majority was so poor. I wished I could do something about it with my limited abilities and resources, at least for poor but meritorious girls, with the help of Jack. I might be able to implement my dream project. I was proud of the friendship of such a noble-hearted man.

At night, I had many things to discuss with Jack.

After dinner at around 11.30 pm I logged in Facebook chat window to see if Jack was available. Yes there he was...

Jack: Honey, are you there? I am waiting for you.

Anindita: Yes Jack, how was your day?

Jack: It's very hectic dear, I am too tired, how are you?

Anindita: A little alright. It's too hot over here, and I had my music class to attend, so I am tired too.

Jack: I wish you could come here, it's so pleasant! Did you have your dinner?

Anindita: Yes. What about you?

Jack: I will have mine after I finish chatting with you.

Anindita: You can go ahead, I would not mind.

Jack: No dear, you don't know how much I enjoy chatting with you. All my exhaustion goes off while talking to you.

Anindita: Really? You always flatter me, however I like it. What will you have in dinner?

Jack: Fried rice and chicken, and some salad. I wish you could serve me, just the very thought gives me much pleasure.

Anindita: In reality, it may never happen. But if you really come to Kolkata I will invite you to my house and serve you nice Indian delicacies.

Jack: Oh! I would long for that opportunity.

Anindita: Jack if you are serious about visiting India, will you have time to visit a few place of interest? I would love to show a few memorable places.

Jack: Yes honey, I will take long leave and we will visit places you want to show me.

Anindita: I will take you to some of my associate NGOs also to show how do I try to help poor people of our society. You would like to visit those places also, won't you?

Jack: Yes honey, as long as you are there with me I will go anywhere.

Anindita: Thank you Jack, you are so kind.

Jack: Don't thank me, it's you who deserves thanks to give me time. I was just shattered after the death of my wife. Now I feel like living longer and love you till the end of my life.

Anindita: Again silly talks! I can't be your life partner, but some day or other you should find a true life partner again and marry.

Jack: Never tell me such a thing ok? I am happy with the relationship we are having. Maybe we would not live together but we can love each other, can't we.

Anindita: You mean platonic love! Sounds great, but in reality it is hard to maintain. I think you are getting late for dinner, please go ahead, we will talk tomorrow afternoon before you leave for site, okay?

Jack: I feel so happy to talk to you, I shall take dinner after sometime.

Anindita: Jack, is it full day for you on Saturday even?

Jack: Yes dear, I told you, I am on contract, so every day is working day.

Anindita: So sad, in any case we will talk for longer time on Sunday, okay? You better log off now and have your dinner, shower, etc.

Jack: Ok honey, I am really hungry now. Bye. Love you.

Anindita: Bye.

I did not notice that Mark Bright was online and had left a message for me. I feel bad, I should have replied to him also.

Anindita: Hi Mark, sorry for the delayed reply. Actually I was reading something, so did not notice you. What are you doing now? Chatting with friends?

Mark: No, I don't have much time for friends, as because I give you time don't think, I do the same for others. I am a businessman; I hardly have spare time.

Anindita: How come I am so fortunate to get your time!

Mark: I told you about my business plans in India. And I found you are quite knowledgeable, so I thought to take your help.

Anindita: Oh no! I am not interested in business. You talk about art, literature, music, I would love to share my thoughts, not business.

Mark: Let me get a drink from fridge.

Anindita: What drink are you having?

Mark: Wine. Would you like some?

Anindita: No thank you. It seems you are already high, better talk to you some other day.

Mark: Oh no Anna, please stay on, and tell me where should I start my project? In Delhi or Mumbai?

Anindita: I don't know how rich you are, but you alone can't do anything in Delhi or Mumbai, that's for sure. You better look for a good consultant else it will be disaster for you, I am sure of it.

Mark: Anna you are not helping me, but you will see that I shall make it.

Anindita: Okay, all the best. Good night. Bye. I logged off.

I wonder what type of businessman he is. Does not have any idea about India but wants to invest, let it be, why should I bother?

Jack and Mark Bright both are based in London but are so different. Both like to continue friendship with me! What have they found in me! I was wondering. I like and have started loving Jack, but Mark Bright did not impress me at all, but let him also be in my friend list, no harm, I told to myself.

Sunday morning has a special effect on our life. Reading four newspapers, having an elaborate breakfast and a special menu for lunch distinguish Sunday from other days.

And now, I have another reason to make it more enjoyable, I plan to chat with Jack in the morning itself because he must have holiday today. So at around 11.30 pm I opened the chat window and wrote a message for Jack, "Good morning dear, hope you are awake by this time, it's around 8 am in London. Hope it will be a holiday for you also. Are you there Jack?"

No, he was not online at that time. But I kept the window open as I knew he would check it sooner or later. Yes, I was right, within fifteen minutes Jack responded,

Jack: Hi honey, very good morning. How are you doing? Hope you had a pleasant sleep. I dreamt of you last night and was so happy to see you beside me.

Anindita: Jack, it's getting too much. Don't indulge in such dreams, it's not good.

Jack: What do I do honey, I love you so much, so I dream of you also.

Anindita: Okay no need to explain things; did you have your breakfast?

Jack: I will have it soon.

Anindita: What will you be taking for breakfast?

Jack: Toast, eggs, fruits and tea, dear.

Anindita: Okay. You should have some milk product also. You know I am a connoisseur of tea, just can't have any tea but good flavored Darjeeling Tea. During my visit to London, I disliked the tea they used to serve at the hotel, it was not at all good

Jack: Did you visit London? When? You did not tell me before. Will you come again please?

Anindita: I have a friend in London, she has given me an open offer to visit London and stay with her, I wish I could visit her, as I have double interest now, I would like to see you also.

Jack: You are most welcome honey. Please do come. I will be so happy to meet you.

Anindita: Really? Only one meeting will make you happy!

Jack: Yes dear, once we meet, we can plan for frequent meetings.

Anindita: Will you invite me to your house at London and introduce me to your mother and daughter?

Jack: Yes dear, they will be delighted to meet you.

Anindita: Actually, I don't have any plans to come to London again but I am surly going to visit Paris in the coming year.

Jack: Honey, we will visit Paris together. By that time my contract will be over and I shall be free. Can I take my daughter along with us?

Anindita: Oh sure, why not. I love children. But don't know if she will like me.

Jack: She will like you I am sure of it. We will have great time together. I am thrilled just by imagining that.

Anindita: But I am sure you would not like to visit Louvre Museum for days together, but my main interest will be to visit that.

Jack: There are so many things to visit in Paris. You must have heard about Love Lock Lake, I will put a love lock there and wish for our everlasting bonding.

Anindita: How romantic! I thought you are a very practical man.

Jack: I am very romantic about our relationship, don't you realize it even now?

Anindita: Yeah I know, but I am not sure about my feelings.

Jack: Honey, you make a detailed plan to visit Paris, how many days we will be there, etc. We will fix our plan accordingly, ok honey.

Anindita: Jack, we are dreaming too much! Now come to the reality. What will happen tomorrow? I am afraid of receiving your parcel, please try to understand. I don't want to be associated with any illegal activity. I want to send it back.

Jack: Honey, why do you think it that way, there is nothing illegal in it. They have arranged the certificate, now it will be safe to receive it.

Anindita: No dear, I don't want that, please try to understand, the whole thing just does not go with my lifestyle, outlook, I don't want to be rich by other's money. Whatever little money I have, I am satisfied with that.

Jack: Honey you are my world now, half of my money is yours, why can't you accept a small token of my love. I am really hurt now.

Anindita: I don't know what to say but I am scared. Since I have accepted your friendship I have to bear its brunt. Let's see what is waiting for me in future. But if there is any problem, hope you will be there to save me.

Jack: Sure honey, I always will be there, don't worry at all. Honey I shall be off now, I have to go to the garage to fix my jeep, it's giving problems.

Anindita: Why should you go? What happened to your driver? He should go.

Jack: No dear, I have to go. The driver is sick, and took leave, so I have to go.

Anindita: I can understand, once an engineer is always an engineer, likes to fix things, be it in big project or a jeep. But before going take your breakfast. Come back soon. If possible, we shall talk at night. Bye.

Jack: Bye Honey.

We logged off.

No matter how much worried I was regarding the parcel, I just knew now that I had no option but to go with the changed situation. It was too hot a day!

The whole day I was unmindful and thinking what to do. I did not want to accept the gifts or money either, but there seemed to be no option but to accept it. The way things were moving now, I couldn't get rid of the problem easily, it was making me sick. But the loving words of Jack made me weak again. I wondered what type of love affair I was getting into, was there such a vacuum in my life! I had fallen for a person who lived in a far-off place, and appeared to be very rich, why should he be involved with me? Is not it very strange! I asked all these questions to myself but did not get any satisfactory answer. I did not feel like opening chat window at night but received a call from Jack saying, "Honey why are you not online? I am missing you, please log in."

Anindita: Jack I am very worried you know, tomorrow your agent will call me for giving me the account number and asking where he should deliver the parcel. I have to take a decision as to whether I should get into a high-risk zone, that question is bothering me so much.

Jack: Honey, I feel sorry for your anxiety, you don't trust me at all. I am telling you not to worry, everything will be done smoothly.

Anindita: Jack, I know the system and procedure of our country better than you and that's why I am so anxious. I don't want to be associated with any illegal activities. Anyway, how do you spend your Sunday evening? Any party?

Jack: No dear, I am not that fortunate. It's a remote place, no club, nothing.

But as long as you are online, I am happy.

Anindita: Now I get it; because of your loveless lonely life you are so much after me.

Jack: Don't insult me this way honey, you may not understand how much I love you, but someday you will regret it.

Anindita: Sorry if I hurt you, actually I am a very emotional person and my love for others often invites trouble in my life, so I am scared now.

Jack: Its ok honey, I do understand. In reality I am still a stranger in your life, but some day or other I will be very much beside you, we are destined to be together.

Anindita: Don't dream too much, better be yourself. Are you having any drink now?

Jack: Yes honey, Irish wine, it's so nice. Wish you could have a little with me.

Anindita: No wonder that makes you so dreamy. You better log off and enjoy your drink. I am sleepy now.

Jack: Ok dear, have a pleasant bed rest and dream of me. I love you so much.

Anindita: Good night. Bye.

Europeans cannot go without drink, and so many varieties were available in the supermarket, as I had seen in London. Even we were tempted to buy a bottle and enjoy it one evening. Their lifestyle is so different but that does not stand as a barrier from loving a person, or so I was thinking. Have I really started loving Jack at this age! Am I a pervert or sinner as they call in religious books? I was not sure. I like to chat with Jack and even with Mark Bright because I do not have any predetermined notion about myself. They are open to discuss many things, which I may not discuss with my Indian friends. In spite of my repeated request, Jack will never call me by my name whereas Mark Bright was so daring that he asked me one day whether I enjoyed sex! I was embarrassed but did not feel shy to admit that in my heydays I enjoyed life. None of my Indian friends would ever ask me such a question; open discussion about sex was a taboo in India. I am really a bit too much daring in my attitude to life. I want to enjoy life as long as I can and want to do something for the society, which has given me so many things to enjoy; on the night that day I was not blessed with sleep, so all these thoughts were pouring in. Actually I was tensed as to how I would face the next day when the parcel arrived!

Day Twelve

It was Monday. In the morning at around 10.30 am, I received a call from Mr John saying, "Madam please check your E-mail, good news awaiting you."

I opened my E-mail and saw a mail from Reserve Bank of India, which read as under:

Dear Customer Anindita K,

Date: 21st April 2014

Time: 2:40 PM

TRANSFER OF ONE HUNDRED THOUSAND POUNDS (VIA RBI)

Regards to the subject matter be informed that we have been instructed and authorized accordingly by (MR JOHN) your agent, based on the approval of the Antiterrorist Fund Certificate–ANTITERRORIST LAW ENFORCEMENT AGENCY UK subdivision and the Financial Services Authority, (FSA) to effect the fund amount of 100,000,00 GBP (ONE HUNDRED THOUSAND POUNDS) through Reserve Bank of India–India's Central Bank within twenty-four working hours.

We have commenced the final process of the approved fund since we have been advised accordingly to transfer the approved fund to your account through RBI and you are required to follow our transfer procedure.

Sequel to this, we require that you make the payment of the transfer service charge (Cost of transaction) of 385,000 INR (THREE LAKH EIGHTY-FIVE THOUSAND RUPEES). This sum can be paid to the department of finance in person, by our Account Officer's account details.

As soon as the payment is made, send a scanned copy of your evidence of payment to our cashier on (customercare@sersindiaonline.in); also send us a copy for our records.

We also require a reconfirmation of your bank details.

We sincerely wish to bring to your kind notice that no part of the required transfer charge (cost of transaction) can be deducted from your fund deposit, which is in a temporary account now in our bank as a bonded fund for the reasons stated below:

– The fund is in a temporary account.

– It is totally insured to its real value.

This is in line with the provisions of section 14 (n) 1 of the Banking Guidelines as adopted in 1993 and modified in 2002 by the ASIA and INDIA Constitutional Bankers Assembly.

As soon as we confirm your payment to our cashier, we shall proceed directly to the transfer of your fund within 3 hours, which will reflect in your account within 24 hours of transfer.

TERMS AND CONDITIONS

PAYMENT

Payment should be made in advance by (RBI) Account Officer's account details to our finance department as stated above.

QUALITY OF SERVICE AND REFUND POLICY

Our transfers are carried out with state-of-the art technology and shall be affected within 24 hours from our confirmation of your payment. Funds transferred normally reflect/ delivered to the destination account/address within twenty-four work hours.

*We look forward to serving you better.

Best regards,

Mrs Sunita Anand

RBI. E-Banking/Online Wire Transfer Department.

RESERVE BANK OF INDIA.

Reserve Bank of India

Central Office

RBI Regional Office 6, Sansad Marg,

New Delhi 110 001, India.

E-mail:remittancedept@sersindiaonline.in

E-mail:customercare@sersindiaonline.in

FOREIGN REMITTANCE DEPARTMENT

Website Link : http://serversrbw-indiaonline.in/online_transction/r

I read the E-mail once, twice, many times just to understand the inner meaning. I wondered what they meant by, "Transfer process has started and it will be reflected in your account within 24 hours, but I have to pay conversion charge upfront!" Wasn't it ridiculous, why could they not adjust charges from the remittances.

I called John to know what he was doing about this. I could not reach him. Instead, I received a SMS from John as:

(21.04.2014 at 9.11) Madam, send your bank account information to my E-mail immediately. Madam, right now I am at the foreign exchange department of Reserve Bank of India, and they are requesting for conversion charges of three lakh eighty-five thousand rupees so that the money will be converted into rupees and remitted into your bank account. I will SMS a bank account for you to make payment.

I SMS back, "Sorry I don't have that much of money in my account, I would not be able to pay. As far as I know, bank deducts charges from the remittance. If RBI doesn't, I can't help."

John: Madam, due to registration, no money can be deducted from the fund and it is too late to go back, because right now your fund has been noted by them and requesting them to cancel the transfer procedure would not be possible.

Anindita: But I can't arrange the sum, you do whatever you like. In the first place, I did not want to get the money.

John: Madam, I have spoken to them and they said that you can make payment of two lakh twenty thousand rupees. Then as soon as the transfer is done, you pay the remaining balance to them. This is the amount they agreed on. The total money of your fund will be around one crore thirteen lakh seven thousand three hundred and fifty-six rupees. Madam, I request you to deposit the minimum charges they are asking for, and then the problem will be solved.

Anindita: How do I make the payment? Give me their account particulars.

John: You cannot deposit the money to their account directly. As agent, I have to deal with that. You remit the sum to the following account: Ansari Reyaz Mansur a/c no: 041005500593 with ICICI Bank, Hyderabad. I shall withdraw money and deposit it to RBI.

Anindita: Why should I deposit money in third party's account? Are you crazy?

John: Madam, yes I have to take a lot of trouble to withdraw money, but there is no other options. I use that account for this purpose alone. You don't worry, you will get proper receipt from RBI once I deposit the sum to them.

Anindita: Listen Mr John, you are compelling me to step into a dark world, I do not appreciate it.

John: Madam, I am taking the trouble for your benefit only and you are blaming me. Why don't you understand the risk I am taking on your behalf?

Anindita: You are pushing me into a risky zone; from the very beginning, I was not willing to accept the illegal pounds.

John: Madam, the question of illegality has been solved and you know that. Now everything will be set right.

Anindita: I am totally confused. I still have my reservation for accepting the money. I shall talk to Mr Smith.

John: Ok madam, you may do so but please remit the sum, otherwise it will be late; there is a time schedule for this transaction, you may have noted.

Anindita: Okay. Let me go to the bank to find out how to arrange the sum. I shall let you know once I can arrange it.

John: Thank you madam. But do it fast.

I was thinking, what should I do? I could arrange the money without the notice of my husband, but should I do that? If RBI puts the money into my account, how do I account for it? I have not seen the person named John, but from his voice, the way he speaks, it appears he is a gentleman, do I have any option but to follow his instruction right now? Should I not go to Delhi and take up the matter with RBI myself? Is there any risk in it? It's a huge sum. If I go alone, would I be able to handle it? Whom should I trust? All these questions were bothering me so much. But time was flitting and I had to pay conversion charge within 24 hours. What do I do? Finally, I thought to follow the instruction of Mr John, as there is not much time and no other options were left to me at that time. I went to my bank, withdrew money, deposited to the account given by John and sent him a SMS that I had completed the transaction.

He replied, "Thank you madam, I shall rush to the bank and withdraw the sum to deposit it to RBI today itself. You will get the receipt of the same by tomorrow. Everything will be completed by tomorrow. Don't worry, madam."

"Thank you Mr John," I replied.

I was thinking of informing this development to Jack during our night chat, as he would be in the project site at the remote place by the Red Sea at the moment. Oh! It was too hot and humid here, unbearable. I tried to take rest putting on the AC in my room. I was very disturbed and restless. I forwarded the E-mail I received from RBI to Jack's E-mail address with a note to go through it and I expressed my inability to deposit the entire conversion charge from my own source, as I did not have that much money in my account. I mentioned also that I had deposited INR 2.2 lakh as per the instruction of the agent.

At night at around 12.30, I opened the chat window of Jack and saw his message:

Jack: Honey, I am online, how are you honey? Hope everything is over.

Anindita: Jack what do you mean by everything is over! Things have started now. I told you I have deposited INR 2.2 lakh from my own source and expecting receipt from RBI by tomorrow, hope they will transfer money by tomorrow.

Jack: Yeah honey, surely they will; you need not worry about the receipt, John will arrange that.

Anindita: Jack, you have put me into so much of trouble. I don't like it at all.

Jack: Honey, I never wanted to put you into trouble, everything will be over by tomorrow. Just relax. Did you have your dinner?

Anindita: Yes it's over. What about you?

Jack: I will have it soon. What did you have at dinner dear?

Anindita: Usual stuff, rice, fish curry, dal, etc. What will you have?

Jack: I don't know what the cook has arranged, may be fried rice and chicken curry. I am so tired, it was a hectic day!

Anindita: Every day of yours seems to be a hectic day.

Jack: Yeah honey, it's really tough. Moreover, my headache also does not leave me.

Anindita: It seems you have a perennial health problem.

Jack: No honey, I had a very sound health but since my wife died last year, I do have some problem.

Anindita: Oh! I am very sorry. But how did she die?

Jack: It was an accident. She was returning from office driving herself and collided with a lorry, someone called me from her mobile. I don't want to remember that night, but since you asked...

Anindita: I am very sorry. I didn't want to hurt you. Please forgive me.

Jack: No, no honey, I did not mind your asking me. I just don't want to recollect those memories.

Anindita: I wonder how do you maintain an ever-smiling face even after going through such plight in life.

Jack: Dear, if we brood over miseries, does it give us any solution? Isn't it better to overcome and enjoy life.

Anindita: Yes, your approach I appreciate, especially when you have a daughter and mother to look after. Do you talk to your daughter often?

Jack: Yes honey, I speak to her every other day.

Anindita: You should be a model father for her. Hope she keeps well and is good at studies.

Jack: Yes she is. Honey, how caring you are! You have a golden heart.

Anindita: Jack I think, it's high time for you to take dinner. We better log off. I will let you know of the developments tomorrow. You could check your E-mail at office, okay?

Jack: Yes honey, the cook is waiting for me. Bye honey, I love you so much.

Anindita: Bye. Have a sound sleep. Good night.

I felt happy after chatting to Jack for so long. He was such a nice person. I couldn't help but love him. I soon went to sleep.

Chapter 2

22nd April 2014

Since morning I was waiting for a call from Mr John regarding the progress of the transfer transaction from RBI. At 10.21 am, I received a SMS, which read: “Good morning madam, check your E-mail for the receipt of your payment, your transfer is in progress now.”

In my E-mail Inbox I found the receipt from RBI as:

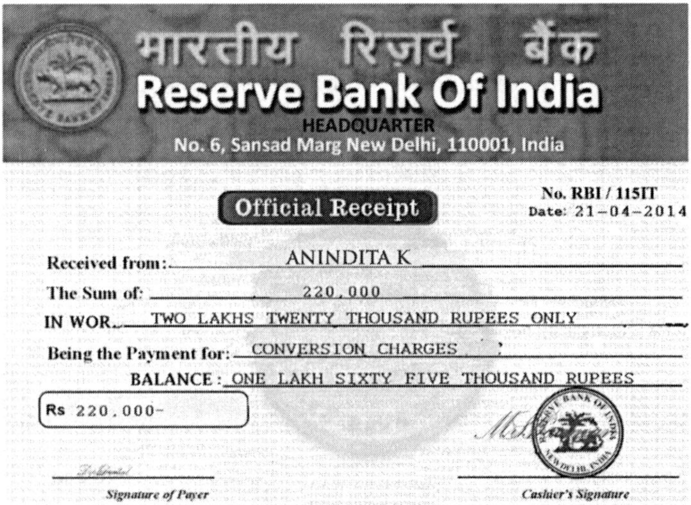
भारतीय रिज़र्व बैंक
Reserve Bank Of India
HEADQUARTER
No. 6, Sansad Marg New Delhi, 110001, India

Official Receipt

No. RBI / 115IT
Date: 21-04-2014

Received from: ANINDITA K
The Sum of: 220,000
IN WOR. TWO LAKHS TWENTY THOUSAND RUPEES ONLY
Being the Payment for: CONVERSION CHARGES
BALANCE: ONE LAKH SIXTY FIVE THOUSAND RUPEES

Rs 220,000-

Signature of Payer

Cashier's Signature

I checked and rechecked the receipt and it appeared to me as a genuine one with RBI symbol, address and date, signature, etc. So, I was a little relieved. But unless the money was deposited into my account, I couldn’t settled down.

To my utter surprise, I received another SMS at 11.28 am from John, which read, “Madam check your E-mail.”

It was another E-mail from RBI claiming CBDT tax as:

ONLINE TRANSFER REMITTANCE DEPARTMENT NEW DELHI.

RESERVE BANK OF INDIA

6, SANSAD MARG, NEW DELHI–110 001 INDIA.

Ref: RBI/EST/678/A08Cdd: 2024/6028/14/311

Swift Codes: CVALESVVXXX

IN LIEU TO THE TRANSFER OF YOUR FUNDS INTO YOUR PERSONAL BANK ACCOUNT.

DEAR CUSTOMER: ANINDITA

WE WANT TO INFORM YOU CONCERNING THE FINAL STAGE OF YOUR TRANSACTION. WE ARE SORRY FOR THE INCONVENIENCES, WHICH WE MIGHT HAVE COST YOU. WE RECEIVED A LETTER THIS MORNING FROM THE (CBDT) MINISTRY OF FINANCE REGARDING YOUR FUND, WHICH IS DUE TO BE TRANSFERRED INTO YOUR ACCOUNT TODAY, AND YOUR TRANSACTION ID WAS FORWARDED TO MINISTRY OF FINANCE FOR REGISTRATION OF THE TAX CLEARANCE CODE AND FINAL APPROVAL.

BUT THEY ARE REQUESTING FOR 9% PERCENT (9%) OF THE TOTAL MONEY, WHICH YOU HAVE TO PAY BEFORE THE REGISTRATION AND APPROVAL WILL BE GRANTED. PLEASE, WE REQUEST YOU TO COOPERATE WITH US TO AVOID KEEPING YOUR TRANSACTION PENDING, WHICH MIGHT LEAD TO CONFISCATING OF YOUR FUND INTO GOVERNMENT’S ACCOUNT. WE ALSO REQUEST YOU

TO CONTACT YOUR TRANSFERRING AGENT MR JOHN REGARDING THIS FOR MORE CLARIFICATION AND ON HOW TO MAKE THIS PAYMENT SO THAT WE CAN TRANSFER WITHIN TWO HOURS.

NOTE: YOU HAVE ONLY 48 HOURS TO COMPLY WITH US, SINCE WE DON'T WANT THIS TRANSACTION TO EXCEED THE TIME, ACCORDING TO INSTRUCTIONS GIVEN TO US BY THE (CBDT) MINISTRY OF FINANCE.

HERE IS THE TOTAL AMOUNT REQUESTED BY MINISTRY OF FINANCE, 912,362.00 INR (NINE LAKH, TWELVE THOUSAND THREE HUNDRED AND SIXTY-TWO RUPEES ONLY), BEING THE 9% PERCENT OF YOUR TOTAL MONEY TO BE TRANSFERRED INTO YOUR GIVEN ACCOUNT.

REGISTRATION AND LEGALIZATION FEE

TAX CHARGES

CLEARANCE FEE

TOTAL SERVICE CHARGES: 912,362.00 INR

We sincerely wish to bring to your kind notice that no part of the required transfer charges (cost of tax) can be deducted from your fund deposit, which is in a temporary account now in our bank as a bonded fund for the reasons stated below;

– The fund is in a temporary account.

– It is totally insured to its real value.

Online Transfer Department/Fund Transfer

Best Regard

E-mail us

remittancedept@sersindiaonline.in

customercare@sersindiaonline.in

I was stunned! I didn't know how to react to this situation. CBTD tax claim might be genuine, but how would I arrange it! I called John and expressed my inability to arrange it.

John: Madam, sender just called me now and asked me to help. I can afford 3.50 lakh madam and you can promise to resend it to me as soon as everything is done.

Anindita: You pay the entire amount or let it be confiscated by Government of India. I can't pay anymore now, I said.

John: I can't do that madam. Do you know what you are saying? You really don't understand what you are saying.

Anindita: I don't have money to pay.

Although I told him that I didn't have money to pay, I was thinking of the possible sources of getting the amount, as I thought the tax component might be a genuine demand from the government. But, why didn't they adjust those charges from the remittance itself? I was wondering about it. But in the E-mail, it was clearly mentioned that it had to be paid upfront. It was so sickening. I opened Facebook chat window and left a message for Jack as I had told him last night to check it in between.

Anindita: Jack be online. I have a serious matter to discuss with you. Now I doubt the integrity of yours as well as the agent you have employed. So far, I have deposited INR 3.5 lakh, but in exchange, I have not received a single thing from the agent. They have taken out the money but why are they not delivering other items to me? How do I believe that I am not being cheated entirely? I have no means to pay the sum RBI is demanding as CBDT. Let the foreign exchange be confiscated by the government. It's not my money, It doesn't bother me.

Few minutes later, Jack responded:

Jack: Honey, I am very sorry to know all this. I never meant this to happen. Honey, try to understand, it has been registered in your name and if you don't pay taxes, government will not permit to release the fund.

Anindita: I can't pay any further. If you are so concerned, why don't you pay the equivalent pounds to the courier company over there and they will instruct their agent to pay it to RBI.

Jack: Honey, I shall try that tomorrow, but I request you not to give up please. Think a little hard, you may also have some source to raise money.

Anindita: No, I do not have. All my money is put in joint names; without the notice of my husband, nothing can be arranged.

Jack: I understand honey, but you should not involve your husband in it. Honey, don't you have jewelry to put in bank and get some loan.

Anindita: How dare you! You should be ashamed to even mention this.

Jack: I am ashamed, no doubt. But just mentioned it in case any other source is not there. I am very upset now. Feeling bad.

Anindita: Your feeling bad is not going to help. You better ask your agent to do something, else I will give up.

Jack: Ok honey, let me think the way out. I am very sorry.

Anindita: If at all I have to pay the taxes, I better go to Delhi and handle the case myself directly with the RBI.

Jack: Honey, never do such a thing. Do not leave your city please. It's election time in your country, anytime anything can happen. Your safety and security will be at stake, let the agent handle the matter, he is an experienced professional man who has dealt with RBI earlier also on behalf of their company.

Anindita: But I hardly know him, neither have I seen him, nor do I know how he looks like.

Jack: Why do you bother about that. You know me and trust me. I will do anything for you, I love you dear.

Anindita: Right now, I require money not love, okay? I am feeling exhausted. No more talking but action is required from your side. Let me log off. I have my music class.

Jack: Ok, honey. Enjoy your lesson and try to compose something for me.

Anindita: Bye.

This Jack was making me mad. I wondered what type of man he was! I enjoyed his loving words and his care for my safety, but how could he dare to tell me to put my jewelry to raise money; I did not like it at all. He had sent me diamond-studded necklace and bangle and Rolex wristwatch; though I was yet to receive the parcel, yet I had seen pictures of those items, and they appeared to be very decent and expensive. "I better ask Mr John to raise money by selling those items and pay the CBDT taxes," I thought.

I had a friend in my music class who used to work at RBI foreign exchange department, so after the class was over, I asked her what was the procedure to receive foreign remittances for charitable purpose. She told me that it was a cumbersome procedure, with lots of formalities to be maintained, so better not to accept it. I could not tell her that I had already entered into the process and it was really getting on my nerves. I became more anxious but didn't know how to solve the problem. If I didn't pay taxes, the government would not give clearances for fund transfer; but how could I arrange for that huge sum? If I gave up, the amount of INR 3.2 lakh, which I had deposited would be forfeited and who knew what next would be there for me, as the money was booked in my name. I felt I was really in great danger. What should I do? Who would guide me? I logged in the RBI site, forex department and searched for the rules and regulations related to foreign exchange. My! It was too much of a reading................ and finally, I could not figure out what exactly would be the charges. My remittance was of unusual type, so I could not find any clear guidelines; I gave up. I was tired also and was not feel like logging in FB chat window. So, I went to sleep early.

I was so anxious that I could not sleep properly, and got up early in the morning and the first question that bothered me was, "What should I do about the tax claim by RBI?" I thought to consult Jack, but at 6 am Indian time it would be midnight at Liverpool, and he would be fast asleep. Even then, I opened the chat window in FB and saw his posting,

Jack: Honey, are you there? Why don't you respond? I am waiting for you for so long, I am missing you. Why didn't you wait for me?

Jack: Honey, what happened to you? Why are you not online dear! You must be knowing how I miss you. Even while I am at work I always remember you, how can you not realize it?

Jack: Honey, this is very bad of you. However, please take care of yourself if you are unwell, just know I love you very much and I have requested the agent to help you settle the financial matter.

Seeing his repeated search last night for my presence online I felt bad, and thought I should not have gone to sleep without chatting with him. However, only I knew how stressful I was right at the moment. How would the agent solve my problem? He would ask me to deposit tax component as early as possible, I already knew that, but how would I get such a huge amount!

At around 10.30 am, Mr John called me on my cell phone and told that last night Mr Smith had asked him to help me. So he had consulted with his wife, who had some money in the bank, and she had agreed to lend it for a short period, and so if I could arrange INR 6 lakh, he would arrange the rest, i.e., INR 3.5 lakh.

Anindita: Mr John I don't like borrowing but I am not in a position to arrange the entire sum, so I have no other way but to accept your proposal. But even then, I am not sure if I could get six lakh as personal loan from bank, I shall try.

John: Madam, please try your level best to arrange the sum today itself and if you could do it, give me a call. I shall instruct you how to deposit it.

Anindita: Okay, thank you for your assistance. Let me see what I could do!

The situation was turning from bad to worse day by day. I was cursing myself and my dear friend Jack also. It was because of his foolish act that I was getting into such trouble. In the unbearable heat outside, I had to go to the bank with my deposit receipts to take loan against that; the very thought made me sick, but I had no respite to come out of the situation I was already in.

On completion of banking formalities, finally, I could get a loan at around 3.30 pm and there was no time to deposit the sum to the accounts Mr John asked me to deposit. In fact, I had a long argument with him regarding depositing CBDT tax. As far as my knowledge went, I knew that for tax deposit a challan was required. I told Mr John that and he assured me that he would do the same for depositing CBDT and would get receipt from RBI. I felt happy and thought of informing Jack of all these developments during our night chat.

I was extremely tired and worried as well, as what was happening during the past four to five days was very unusual and I could not consult anybody about it. Jack was very busy throughout the day in a far-off place and his loving words during chat I did like without a doubt, but sometimes I detested it also. I decided to tell him that.

I opened Facebook chat window, and Jack was there...

Jack: Honey, how are you doing my angel?

Anindita: Please stop calling me by all these. I am very upset because of your foolish act and you are asking me if I am fine.

Jack: Honey, I am really very sorry. I asked the agent to help you, hope he solved your problem to some extent.

Anindita: But I don't like it at all. How would you realize what is going on in my mind? I hate borrowing, but I had to agree with the agent's proposal. I had no other source of money.

Jack: Honey, I do understand, I just want everything to be over. I am really worried my angel. I never meant it this way. Hope on receipt of taxes, RBI will release the remittances.

Anindita: If they don't and demand something else, what will you do?

Jack: I will break my contract with the company and surly will come down to India to help you.

Anindita: You can't do that I know very well. Don't make a false promise, okay.

Jack: Honey, you are very angry with me, but just know I love you so much.

Anindita: What I will do with your love, which brings so much of stress in my life! I detest it.

Jack: Honey, never say such words please. Love is made in heaven, it's a blessing of God.

Anindita: I told you I am not a believer. Listen, I am not in love with you, I consider you as a far-off friend may be.

Jack: Ok Honey, I will make you believe when we will meet.

Anindita: Okay, you go on dreaming. I know very well those days will never come.

Anindita: Jack, I am really tired, want to go to bed. We better log off.

Jack: Ok honey, have pleasant bed rest, dream of me. I shall dream of you also. Bye.

We logged off. I went to sleep. It was 2 a.m. in India.

23rd April, 2014

I could not sleep the previous night. It was very hot and humid, and my mind was restless as I had parted with six lakh rupees towards payment of CBDT and Mr John was supposed to deposit it to RBI. I was expecting a call or SMS from him and receipt of my payment. Unless I got it, I wouldn't be able to take my breakfast also. Time and again I was looking at the wall clock as to when the office time would start and I would get the deposit receipt from RBI.

Mr John called me at 11 pm.

John: Mam, I have deposited the money. You will get receipt in E-mail soon. I tried to help you as per request of Mr Smith. I have taken INR 3.5 lakh from my wife and paid entire CBDT to RBI. As soon as they release your remittance, you should pay me back my wife's money and buy me a nice wine as my fees. It was really a very tough time for me. My wife really helped.

Anindita: Okay Mr John, thanks for the trouble you have taken. I still wish that such legalizing wouldn't have taken place and that you had returned those GBP at the very beginning. However, when will RBI release the remittances, any idea?

John: By tomorrow, I suppose.

Anindita: Not sure or what?

John: They have some official procedure to maintain, so it may take a day.

Anindita: That means I have to bear the tension for one more day!

John: Madam, take it easy. The tax is deposited; now they are bound to release the fund to your account.

Anindita: I am not so sure. You never told me before about the tax component. I doubt if you really know the rules and regulations of RBI.

John: Madam, why don't you trust me. I have invested my money also. Do you think I am doing this for nothing?

Anindita: Okay, I don't want to argue, only wish to get the fund so that our expenses are squared off. Bye.

We were exchanging SMS.

At around 2 pm, I received E-receipt of CBDT from RBI. I was happy to some extent.

On that day, I had a party to attend in the evening; I went to a club to meet my university friends. Once in a month we met and enjoy the company of old friends, and had dinner together; it used to be a very enjoyable day for all of us. But my mind was not free that day, so I could not enjoy it whole heartedly. I could not share my love story with them but

I was feeling good among my old friends just by thinking that at this age when most of my middle-aged friends had lost their physical charm, I could maintain my physic so well that a person of a far-off place could fall for me! Another thing made me happy; during our *adda*, someone told that nowadays even our judiciary system had accepted E-mailing as medium of communication to save paperwork and to support the Go Green Movement. It was an affirmation to me, as I was a little apprehensive about the receipt of deposit from RBI through E-mail. I thought that even RBI might have taken the same policy to reduce paperwork. I returned home at around 10 pm; I had so many things regarding which to chat with Jack, so opened FB chat.

I saw Jack was waiting for me to log in.

Jack: Honey, are you there? I am waiting for you since afternoon. You did not leave any message for me. What has happened with RBI tax deposit?

Anindita: Yes Mr Smith, I have just come back from a social gathering with friends.

Jack: What was that? You are so lucky to have so many friends.

Anindita: Friendship is to be maintained, I like it.

Jack: Yes dear, you are a good-hearted person. I love you so much. Now tell me, did the agent help you?

Anindita: Yes he did, I received E-receipt from RBI for the CBDT. Now it is to see when they will release the fund.

Jack: Oh thank God, I am so happy now. I think things will be settled soon.

Anindita: Hope for the best. How was your day?

Jack: Very tiring. Onshore work is going to be completed within few days, toughest part will start by next week or so.

Anindita: What is that?

Jack: We have to work under the sea. I don't know how I will maintain communication with you from there.

Anindita: Oh my God! But for such a huge project you must have use of net service also.

Jack: Yes but signaling may be a problem, I am not so sure.

Anindita: Very bad, but before going there you must inform me, else I will be very anxious about you.

Jack: Sure dear, I will go mad if I don't get a chance to chat with you. How are you keeping tonight?

Anindita: Fine for once, as I met my old friends, had nice dinner, wonderful evening.

Jack: It seems you did not miss me at all. I missed you so much.

Anindita: Do you think I have any respite but to think about you! The problem you have put me into keeps me worried all the time.

Jack: Honey, everything is over now. Why do you worry? By tomorrow you will get the entire sum I believe.

Anindita: I can't be that optimistic, let's see. Let's talk about something else, I feel sick of discussing this money matter all the time. Tell me do you have those puppies I have seen in your photo post, still at home? They are lovely.

Jack: Yes dear, I will give you a puppy when I will be in India.

Anindita: No thank you, we used to have doggies, but they are too much of bonding, restricts our movements. I no longer keep any pet, as I want to travel a lot. I should be free.

Jack: Ok dear, I understand. We shall be traveling together and shall see places.

Anindita: How do you indulge in such daydreaming? Must be tired and hungry. Please go ahead and take your dinner, shower, and go to sleep.

Jack: Yes dear, I am famished. I will miss you. But nothing can stop me to love you. I love you so much. Bye dear.

Anindita: Bye.

We logged off.

But Mark Bright was online and posted a message for me. So I opened his window.

Mark: Hi Anna, why don't you respond to my call? I have many things to discuss with you.

Anindita: I was a little busy. Okay, tell me, how can I help you?

Mark: You know I am planning to visit your country in the early part of next month to set up my project.

Anindita: It will be too hot over here. I think for the project you have to do lot of surveys, meet people, it will be difficult for you in summer.

Mark: Oh no, I was in Dubai last year around, same time. Dubai is the hottest place in the world, I suppose. Now tell me, which city of your country will be good for my venture?

Anindita: I told you earlier also that I have no knowledge in this line. But I only know it is very difficult to acquire land in megacities like Mumbai and Delhi. You better try for Bangalore, Hyderabad, Gurgoan, etc., which are growing fast.

Mark: Someone told me to invest in Delhi.

Anindita: If you have source you may try. I am not very sure.

Mark: Ok, let me find out what are the possibilities. But we should meet when I am in your country.

Anindita: How? Do you mean to say that I will be coming to meet you in Delhi? It would not be possible for me, especially it being election time in our country. If you come to Kolkata, I may think, but that is also not a very good proposition. Virtual friends should remain in one's imagination, meeting will spoil the game.

Mark: Why do you think so? Do you think anything can happen between us?

Anindita: No, nothing will happen, only our illusion will be shattered.

Mark: Even then, I will take the risk. I really want to meet you.

Anindita: You people are very funny. Why do you want to meet me? I can't be any help for your business, not even in your personal finding of life partner.

Mark: Ha ha...you are afraid of meeting me, surely you have some feeling for me.

Anindita: I am getting tired, it is midnight, I don't want to chat on for no issue, good night.

Mark: Ok Anna, once I finalize my plan, I will let you know. I have to apply for visa, book tickets, make plans, lot of things to do. It will keep me busy next week.

Anindita: It seems you are serious about your venture, okay. Wish you all the best.

Mark: Thank you dear Anna, we will meet soon. Good night.

Anindita: Good night.

We logged off. I was amazed no doubt. Why do these people want to meet me? I really didn't have that level of curiosity about them, I just enjoyed chatting with them. It was a new way of passing my lonely time. Was I doing anything wrong? Was I giving any wrong impression about myself? I asked to myself, but really I couldn't find any flaws on my part. I had told both Jack and Mark that I was a married woman, having loving family and enjoying life! Even then, why had they approached me this way? I was very annoyed with myself for indulging in such a relationship! Did I really indulge them? I should be more careful in the future, I thought. With thinking all such rubbish, I went to sleep.

24th April 2014

This year summer appeared to be unbearable, and my mind was also restless because of the RBI remittance issue. When will they release the fund? Already I had spent a few lakhs, and I owed INR 3.5 lakh to Mr John. I was feeling extremely bad. I wanted to return his money as early as possible. If RBI didn't release the money today, again the weekend would come and I would have to wait with anxiety till Monday. I thought to visit the local RBI to know the actual system and procedure, but due to the crouching heat outside, I abandoned that plan. I checked E-mail, time and again, but except some promotional mail, nothing important was there. I talked to my son through G-talk. He was supposed to visit us during May, summer vacation time, and stay with us for a month, but he again said that it might be postponed till the end of June as he had to complete an assignment, which may take a month or so. I was unhappy about his schedule but at the same time a little relieved as I hoped all the problems related to this remittances would be settled down by that time and I would be free to enjoy his company at home. I missed him very much. I was wondering how I could manage to chat with Jack when Jeet, my son would be at home! Of course, I had a net connected Android cell phone, so it would be possible to maintain my night chat through cell, I thought. Anyway, I had to consult Jack to maintain a fixed time for chatting.

At night, I once again opened FB chat to see if Jack was available and saw his posting:

Jack: How are you doing my angel? Hope you are keeping well. I was missing you and was anxious to know what has happened today, did RBI release the fund honey?

Anindita: No they have not, I am so anxious.

Jack: This is very bad honey! I wonder why they are taking so long? Hope it will be settled by tomorrow.

Anindita: Yes I hope so, but if they don't, we have to wait till Monday as there will be no forex transaction on Saturday.

Jack: Honey, everything will be over by tomorrow. Honey, what did you do during the day? Did you have your music class?

Anindita: No, I will be going tomorrow. It is so hot here. Just sitting inside an AC room with lot of tension about your money.

Jack: It's all yours dear, not mine.

Anindita: That is true. I have not seen a single rupee till now but have spent so much amount!

Jack: Honey, I am very sorry. Had I known that the procedure was so cumbersome, I never would have put you into this trouble. Now we just can't quit.

Anindita: I don't want to think over it anymore. I have my personal problem also. My son will be coming home by end of May. I am planning an outing with him, may be in some hilly place to enjoy the cool weather.

Jack: Really? Where do you plan to visit?

Anindita: May be Kashmir, which is known as Heaven on Earth..

Jack: As far as I know, it is a disturbed place in India. Am I right?

Anindita: Yes, it used to be, but nowadays our government has taken measures to safeguard the place and encourage tourism, so it will be okay I think.

Jack: Dear, even then you should not take the risk.

Anindita: You must have heard the name of the writer Salman Rushdie. I am a great admirer of his books, I liked his book Shalimar the Clown. It's on Kashmir and its people. He is a very powerful writer. Do you know he lives in London, almost confined to house, as hardcore Muslims are after his life!

Jack: No, I did not know. Dear, you really read a lot! I hardly get time to read.

Anindita: Reading is a habit. if anyone develops it, I bet one can't just go without it. Anyway, I think you are getting late for your dinner. Let's log off. I am also feeling sleepy. Will let you know the developments of tomorrow. Bye.

Jack: Bye honey. Have a good bed rest. I love you so much.

25th April 2014 (Friday)

I was checking my account where RBI was supposed to credit the sum but it was in vain! No money was deposited there and I was afraid of the consequences, were they going to claim some other charges! Why were they delaying the transfer? All these question were in my mind but I could not ask anyone. I thought to call Mr John but did not feel like it, as I knew he did not have the authority to release the money. Ultimately, at around 1 pm, Mr John SMS me to open my E-mail. I apprehended that and saw a mail from RBI claiming IMF charges of INR 5 lakh within 48 hours. I was furious and decided not to comply with the demand anymore no matter what may happen to the money I had already spend all I could. I immediately called Mr John and conveyed my decision to him.

John: Madam, you can't quit at this stage you must be knowing. Unless you pay their charges, RBI will not release the fund. Earlier charges whatever we have paid so far will be forfeited. I am anxious to get back my money, which is urgently required for paying an installment of loan we had taken for housing purpose.

Anindita: It's you who dragged me to this problem; however, I am undone. Let me talk to Jack, if he could arrange anything to pay the charges then only you can get back your money.

John: Madam, I am a poor person living with children. That money was my lifetime saving for housing purpose. I want to get it back as early as possible.

Anindita: In that case, why don't you negotiate with RBI official to adjust the charge from the converted fund and release the rest of the amount.

John: Madam, they have clearly mentioned in their E-mail that it can't be done. Have you not read it?

Anindita: Yes, I have read it but can't understand head or tail of the rule they have referred to. However, I don't want to argue with you on the issue. I am undone. I have no means to pay the charge.

John: Madam, you have to arrange it, try to understand, else both you and me will lose everything.

Anindita: I do understand but would not be able to arrange a single rupee. Bye.

I switched off my cell in disgust. What should I do now? Why this IMF charge at all? What function IMF had to do in this transaction? Whom should I ask? Local RBI?

I had decided to do that but it couldn't be done before Monday. The next day was Saturday, and RBI would be closed to the public. So I had to wait till Monday. I hated Jack for throwing me into such trouble. "Jack I hate you, I hate you," I was telling repeatedly. Today I had my music class to attend but in such mental condition, how could I go there? The whole thing made me sick. I was crying alone; no one was there to consult or console me either. I did not feel like opening the chat window even, as I knew Jack would be in his site, far-off from his office. But I had to let him know the developments, so I opened chat window. To my utter surprise, I saw that Jack was online.

Jack: Honey, are you there? The agent just called me. He is on my neck to get back his money. I don't know what to say.

Anindita: If you don't know, who will know? I am undone.

John: This is really very bad honey. If there is any way to transfer money from here, I could have done so immediately.

Anindita: This weekend you go to London, as you said it's a four-hour journey only, arrange to remit fund through proper banking channel and solve the problem.

Jack: Honey, I would love to do that but if I leave the station the company will sue me, I will lose the job and will be delisted. Better forget everything. I feel like killing myself.

Anindita: The problem will not be solved if you kill yourself. Your agent is a useless person, I always doubted his integrity. I am really helpless now. What will happen if I could not pay the IMF charge?

Jack: Honey, the entire amount will be transferred to dormant account I suppose.

Anindita: Fine. Let it be in dormant account of RBI. If you ever come to India as sender you may claim that amount. And pay back my expenses only.

Jack: Honey, it will be too late then and the procedure will be much more cumbersome.

Anindita: Then what do you suggest?

Jack: Honey, I dare not to suggest you anything. I have put you in such a stress, I am ashamed of it. You think over, and if you find any solution I will be happy.

Anindita: Solution means I have to arrange to pay the charge? Not possible. I better go to local RBI with copies of all the E-mails sent by them just to know what are the charges one is required to pay for getting any inward remittances.

Jack: Oh no honey, don't do that. They will not be of any help, rather they will claim local charge from you.

Anindita: How do you know that? This government agency must have set rules, which I want to know.

Jack: Honey, I am sure there will be no other charges after this IMF one.

Anindita: You never know. However, let me think if I can arrange the sum. All my money will be at stake because of you.

Jack: Honey, don't worry about your expenses. I will replenish you in the very first chance, believe me, you are my love, my world. I can do anything for you.

Anindita: Yes, you can make my life hell that's for sure.

Jack: Honey, you are hurting me, ok I deserve it. But I love you so much and will love you till the end of my life.

Anindita: I hate to hear such vague words. You can't show your love right now and you are promising me love till the end of your life! You people are not dependable at all. I made a great mistake by accepting your friend request.

Jack: Honey, you are making me cry. You insult me as much as you want but be my friend forever, ok?

Anindita: Jack I am tired. Don't feel like talking anymore. Bye.

I logged off the chat window.

I really didn't know what to do next? I was an independent person. I didn't need to consult anybody for taking any decision of my life. My husband hardly interfered in my activities. My son was a scholar, and did not need my support anymore. We were not rich, but were financially sound. As a result, from the very beginning, I was reluctant to accept the fund Jack dispatched for me. But the situation compelled me to get into the deal and now I was quite helpless. Neither could I consult anybody nor could I just give up. Already so much money I had been spent out of my own deposits, and the way things were moving, I doubted the number of charges there would be, before RBI released the fund. Now I realized why my music class friend, ex-employee of RBI, had told me not to accept it. Even I wanted to return it but Jack had almost begged me to accept it and I had no way but to go ahead. Was I not a greedy person for such a huge fortune, which came my way all of a sudden? I asked myself. Actually,

I was not greedy for the wealth but for the friendship of Jack, chatting with him gave me so much of pleasure! His six feet four inches tall figure and smiling face holding his daughter on his lap and picture of his pet dogs all had a magical effect on me, I just loved them.

On the other hand, Mark Bright had not impressed me at all. But he was very fast in his decision making. I was surprised to see his fast movements. He really meant to do some business in India! It was better that he be at Mumbai. Hopefully he might not come all the way to Kolkata to see me, I thought. I hardly exchanged any personal information with him but he seemed to be very keen to know my likes and dislikes. From his profile, I had gathered that he was a medium height, well-built, fair Irish man of middle age. Since I looked younger at my age, both Jack and Mark were impressed by my profile picture. But I warned them repeatedly that I may be older to them, could be a good friend but not a life partner! So I was very clear about my conscious.

I was thinking all these lying on my bed on Saturday night, as sleep did not favor me due to my anxiety about the IMF charge. From where would I get lakhs of rupees all the time! RBI was demanding everything in lakhs not in thousands! Too much for me. I was going to become mad.

Sunday morning was never so bad for me. I had a severe headache due to the sleepless night and it was too hot and humid; with every single movement, I was sweating like a dog! I decided to meditate for some time to ease my tension. But at around 11.30 am, I could not help but opened Facebook chat window just to see if Jack was awake, it might be early morning at Liverpool.

Jack was not online, but I left a note for him, "Good morning dear. Last night was a nightmare for me, I could not sleep and had a severe headache, should take rest during daytime. However, I want to forget everything, I have decided not to pay anymore. Don't bother me anymore." After posting these words, I logged off. I decided to go for shopping and have lunch outside. The past few days were really tiring and the RBI episode had kept bothering me for long. I was not going to oblige them further, let what may come in the future. I was consoling myself. I went to City Mall, did window shopping mostly, as I hardly had anything to buy. I didn't like dumping things in my house with useless items but I wanted to buy a few books, as for long I was not reading any good book. So I went to Star Mark, bought few books and took lunch at food court. Feeling happy, I returned home in the evening. I tried to forget everything as if nothing unusual had happened in my life. I was lying on bed with new books when I received a call from Jack saying: "Honey why don't you log on to chat window, I am waiting for you for so long?"

Anindita: You must have seen my note, I am not well.

Jack: Yes honey, that makes me more worried, how are you now dear?

Anindita: Ok.

Jack: Honey, please be online. I have so many things to discuss with you.

Anindita: Jack after many days, I am feeling little relieved, please don't spoil my mood okay?

Jack: Yes dear, I never think of spoiling your mood. I love you dear.

I logged in chat window and saw that Jack had posted.

Jack: Honey, last night I also could not sleep, thinking how could I help you.

Anindita: Please don't try to help me anymore, I just want to give up the whole thing.

Jack: Honey, please try to put yourselves in my shoes and realize how you will feel if someone you love from the core of your heart just refuses to listen to you? Honey, if you do not listen to me, who will listen? Don't you love me a bit? Value my friendship a little? If yes, then please listen to me for the last time, please try to arrange IMF charges if you can. I will not insist of you, but if you can't arrange, I have to think of alternative ways. I may have to break my contract with the company by paying heavy penalties and come down to India to solve the problem.

Anindita: Hey, don't play with my emotions.

Jack: I am serious about you and don't want to put you in hardship anymore. But I am not sure if I will get visa so soon; moreover, if I break my contract, company will sue me, I may not get visa even.

Anindita- So back to square one, I have to arrange money!

Jack: Honey, if you can I will be most happy and believe me I will refund you all the expenses you have incurred so far at first chance. You are my world, you are my love; how could I bear your suffering for me?

Anindita: Enough is enough, I am not flattered with your love song, but I do value your friendship so I may give a last try tomorrow.

Jack: Oh honey, you are a gem of a person, I am relieved! Honey, do you know my condition? Since morning, right after breakfast, I was having a meeting with group of engineers and with my boss, planning our undersea project. Last night was also very bad for me, no sleep. I am sandwiched with work pressure and tension related to your RBI remittances.

Anindita: Poor things! Do you want that I should sympathize with you? No way, you have dug your own grave, how can anyone help you?

Jack: Honey, don't say so, I expect a little mental support from you dear. If I know that your problem is solved, half of my tension will be over. In my field of work, I will manage things with my skill.

Anindita: Okay I understand, however aren't you going to enjoy drinks with friends this Sunday evening?

Jack: No dear, I am having some wine sitting alone in my lodge as there are no friends around. But you are here with me.

Anindita: Jack, your platonic love also makes me weak.

Jack: Really? I am honored. Someday, I believe we will live together.

Anindita: How? I am not interested to relocate.

Jack: Once you meet me your opinion may change.

Anindita: What do you think, I am impressed by your riches, or by your educational background or by your well-built 6.4 feet body and charming smile?

Jack: Well said, I am a combination of all these, will you not be impressed by any of these?

Anindita: Not at all. If you are a good person at heart only then I will be delighted.

Jack: I am a good person. And given my heart to you, now you decide what you will do with that.

Anindita: Jack you are too much! These romantic conversations! How many times you have uttered them in your life? Nice to hear it, even if it is false.

Jack: It's not false dear, you will realize it someday.

Anindita: Okay, I think you are a little high now. Good night Jack.

Jack: Is it very late at night there?

Anindita: Yes, I should go to sleep.

Jack: Ok dear, good night then. Sleep well and dream of me.

Anindita: Good night.

I logged off his window but Mark Bright was pining me for quite some time. So I had opened his chat window.

Mark: Hi, Anna, you are online but not responding to my call! You know I have applied for visa to India.

Anindita: My! You are so fast! When do you plan to come?

Mark: This month end. It seems you have not opened your mail, I have forwarded a copy of return air tickets from Heathrow to Mumbai booked in British Airways, departure dated 28th May and return 13th June, to your mailbox.

Anindita: What shall I do with your tickets?

Mark: You will trust me. So far, we had chats now I want to make a real move.

Anindita: Move means with your business plan I suppose.

Mark: Yes my business plan, and my plan to meet you.

Anindita: Where do you decide to start your project?

Mark: I will be going to Mumbai first and then to Delhi.

Anindita: Okay, nice hearing your planning. I wish you all the success.

Mark: Hey only wish will not do, you have to meet me. I will be coming to Kolkata to see you.

Anindita: My! Why do you want that, our virtual friendship is far enjoyable to the actual meeting. You may be disillusioned.

Mark: Anna, I want to meet you. I have found a good woman inside you who could guide me in many things, please let me meet you, ok?

Anindita: You surprise me no doubt. Within few days of virtual friendship how do you find things in me to depend on?

Mark: Anna, I am a businessman, I can read people's mind quickly.

Anindita: Really? Through chatting only how do you study my nature, I wonder.

Mark: I hardly misjudge people. You are a very dependable friend.

Anindita: Thanks. It's getting late. I am sleepy. We shall talk some other day. Good night.

Mark: Good night my sweet and dear friend.

Oh God! Finally, I could get rid of my far-off friends. I really enjoyed chatting with them. That night I was feeling tired and happy also. Both my virtual friends were so keen to meet me, which was quite surprising. These rich people might spend a lot of money just like that! I opened my E-mail and found Mark's forwarded air ticket and wondered why he was moving so fast! However, it was high time to go to bed, as it had passed quarter to 1 pm.

Monday morning started with my plan to find out ways to arrange for IMF charges. I really felt like running away and hide somewhere so that all the problems would not bother me. Should I keep my mobile switched off and never open G-mail, or Facebook, so that I would get rid of the problem! I was asking myself and again I knew that was not possible, I had no escape. Finally, I arranged money by pledging my gold ornaments to the bank. It took two days for me to get the money and to deposit the sum in some odd accounts as per instruction of Mr John. I requested him to follow-up with RBI for releasing the fund to my account. He assured me that it would be done within 24 hours. I received deposit receipt from RBI through E-mail, was relieved to some extent, and again was waiting to see credit into my account. At night, I chatted with Jack.

Jack: Honey, how are you doing? Hope everything is over.

Anindita: Jack, what do you mean by that? I have not received money into my account yet, unless that is done, I am finished.

Jack: Honey, don't be worried, it will end soon. I am so glad that you could arrange money.

Anindita: With the hope that RBI will release the fund now, but if they don't and ask for some other charge, what shall I do?

Jack: No, they can't ask for any other charge. I am sure they will release the fund now.

Anindita: Let's see, I have crossed my fingers. Not feeling well at all. Anyway, how was your day?

Jack: Honey, I am really under pressure. Our underwater project will start soon, so many things to do now. No time to look back.

Anindita: That means if I need your help to solve my problem you will not be available.

Jack: Honey, I will always be there for you. Just know I love you so much.

Anindita: Your love will not be any help in crisis I know. Listen I don't like the way Mr John is insisting on me to deposit money in some odd accounts, I really don't understand why he is doing this.

Jack: Honey, he handles so many cases like this, you don't worry about the procedure; it's their business, they know how to handle it.

Anindita: May be you are right, but I am so much worried! I have spent so much money but so far nothing has come to my account.

Jack: Honey, there is no concept of partial credit; RBI will release the entire sum at a time, you just keep patience, ok honey?

Anindita: Yes I have no other option but to wait and see.

Jack: Honey, I am telling you do not worry about your expenses, I shall replenish it. Please keep faith in me.

Anindita: Okay dear, you may be a rich person, but I have very small means, so I can't bear such a risk for long.

Jack: I understand, I am really sorry for putting you to such trouble. But it will be over very soon, trust me.

Anindita: Jack, it's very late at night, we should log off, it's so hot and humid over here. I don't know if I will be able to sleep at all.

Jack: Ok honey, I am also famished, Good night. Love you so much.

Anindita: Bye.

We logged off. Fortunately, Mark Bright was not there online for the past few days after sending his air tickets. I wondered what he was planning for his business trip! Let him do whatever he likes, I couldn't take much pressure at the moment. I went to bed, but as usual I could not sleep throughout the night.

Nothing happened the next day. I was checking my accounts in vain, no fund transfer from RBI! And to my utter surprise, I received an E-mail from RBI, which stated that due to delay in paying IMF charges, I had to pay demurrage charges or else my account couldn't be activated! And those demurrage charges of INR 3.8 lakh were also to be paid within 48 hours. Mr John called me and stated that he tried his best to convince RBI officials to waive this demurrage charge but they expressed their inability as it was related to IMF for which they have no discretionary powers. He asked me to arrange the charges within the timeframe, otherwise, some more charges would be added. I did not know how to react to this situation, my brain was not working. There was no use of arguing with Mr John as he was a mere middle man. Neither Jack could come up with any help as he was already very much busy with his project. Whatever I would tell, he would express his concern about my stress but could not help me with further remittance right at the moment, which was very clear from our Sunday night conversation. So I was thinking what to do. I SMS to Mr John asking if he could sell off those jewelry lying with them and arrange money. He replied that their company couldn't do that as they are mere custodian of those items for the time being. Once the fund was released they were bound to deliver those items to me. I found no way to solve the troubled situation. It was very clear to me, either I pay or I forget the money I had already spent. Even then, I might not be excused, as so many government agencies were already involved in the whole process. So I had to find ways to raise money somehow.

At night, I logged in Facebook chat window to converse with Jack. But he was not there. I did not wait for long as I knew it would be the same old helpless conversations. He would feel bad to hear the developments but would not be able to do anything to reduce my burden. I logged off.

I was in dilemma as to whether I should again try to raise money as I did not have any other personal savings left now. If I had to arrange money I had to take it from my family saving for which consent of my husband and son might be required. That was not a feasible solution, but what could I do! The more I thought, the more I got sick. Moreover, the heat of the summer made my condition unbearable. Finally, I took the decision to visit my bank with all deposit receipts and request for overdraft limit against those.

Accordingly, next day I visited my bank and convinced the manager to grant me overdraft against the deposit receipts based on my application, being the first account holder, with the promise to complete formalities related to documentations as soon as my husband and son would be back in Kolkata. I made that move with the hope that RBI would not hold back the fund for long. If I paid the charges on time they were bound to release the fund. I was happy that within 24 hours I could arrange the money and remit it to an account as per instruction of Mr John. He thanked me again and again for my cooperation. And I asked him to follow-up with RBI. After completing all those tiring processes, I came back home at around 4.30 p.m. and received a call from Jack to log on FB. I was so tired but just could not ignore his request, as last night I did not wait for him to log in.

"Honey, why did not you wait for me last night," was his first bouncer!

Anindita: Do you expect me to wait for time immemorial?

Jack: Honey, my jeep broke down. It took so long to fix, I was late, and upset as well when I saw you were not there. Honey, hope you are keeping well.

Anindita: No, I can't keep well as long as I do not get fund from RBI. I have spent lakhs of Indian rupees but not yet received a single rupee.

Jack: Oh my God ! Have they not yet released the fund, I thought everything is over and they must have released the fund.

Anindita: It seems you are not aware of the latest development. RBI claimed demurrage charge for late payment of IMF charge.

Jack: What! I can't believe it, do you mean it or joking with me dear?

Anindita: No, I am not joking. I am finished Jack.

Jack: Honey, why all these are happening to us? I never meant to give you any stress at all. I wanted to help you for your NGO, but RBI formalities appear to be very cumbersome.

Anindita: I don't know. I still have doubt if agent John is a right man to handle such cases.

Jack: Honey, I shall talk to their Head Office if they can take up things directly with RBI.

Anindita: Do whatever you like. I can't bear this stress any further.

Jack: I understand honey. Thinking about your stress I am also getting sick, please bear for some more time, we will find some solution very soon.

Anindita: When are you going to start your undersea project?

Jack: Any day dear.

Anindita: How will be your life under the sea? Very thrilling, I suppose.

Jack: No honey. We have to work day and night and I am not very well also.

Anindita: What has happened to you?

Jack: Same old problem of severe headache, don't feel like eating anything also.

Anindita: I am very sorry to know this. Have you consulted any doctor?

Jack: No dear, did not get time. I shall visit doctor in the weekend.

Anindita: That would not be wise, visit doctor tomorrow itself. You are having so many responsibilities you should remain well.

Jack: Thank you so much for your concern about me. I am honored. I wish you could be beside me that would have reduced all my pain.

Anindita: Ha ha, you are daydreaming! However, let me tell you one thing, I do not like your this formal profile picture at all, would you please change it to an informal picture? I want to see you, could you Skype please?

Jack: Dear, I would love to talk to you on Skype but not today please, I am really sick, want to take rest. Ok I shall change my profile picture as you wish. We shall Skype some other day dear, ok?

Anindita: Okay. Take rest. Good night.

Jack: Good night honey. Just know I love you so much.

We logged off. No matter how much stressful I was because of Jack's foolish act, I enjoyed his presence at FB.

Human mind is so unpredictable! I did not understand why I was so concerned about far-off friends on Facebook! Mark Bright was not coming online for few days, why? He was supposed to discuss his travel plans to India with me but conspicuously he was not available in Facebook; must be he was busy with his business activities, but I missed him also. Chatting with him gave me some relief from the long summer night and stress related to RBI remittances.

So I opened his personal chat window and wrote, "Mark, you were supposed to discuss with me details of your plan related to your visit to India but you are not online for few days, is it not an insult to me? I am really angry with you." And finally, I retired to bed that night.

Next day morning I realized that there was no possibility to release the fund by RBI within the week as there was a national holiday, followed by Saturday, Sunday, and Lok Sabha Election Day in our state on Monday. I was anxious and happy at the same time as I thought that I would not need to access my bank account to verify if money had been deposited there or not. So I had free time to do things and enjoy as per my wish. I attended Tagore's birthday celebration function at our local library, sang a song even, and was very much happy. As usual at night I chatted with Jack.

Jack: Honey, how are you?

Anindita: I am fine, you know I remain happy when I am associated with cultural activities. Today we were celebrating birthday of our great poet Rabindranath Tagore and there were a lot of cultural programs, even I sang a song.

Jack: Really? I am so happy to know that you enjoyed your day. When are you going to compose a song for me?

Anindita: Hey don't think I am so great that I could compose song for you but I shall give it a try some other day after the RBI problem is over.

Jack: Honey, it will be over by next week.

Anindita: I hope so also. How was your day?

Jack: There was marathon meeting on our next part of projects with all engineers and bosses. I am under tremendous pressure.

Aniita: Poor thing! How is your health, I mean headache?

Jack: It's still there, I have learnt to live with that.

Anindita: So sad. It's not a good sign at all. Consult a doctor as early as possible.

Jack: Yes dear, I shall. How is weather in your place now? If it is still very hot, take good care of yourself, do not go outside. Drink plenty of water.

Anindita: Thanks for your concern. You must be tired, please have your dinner, shower, etc., I don't want to delay you.

Jack: Ok honey, though I enjoy chatting to you but now I should retire to bed early. Lots of work tomorrow. Bye honey. I love you so much.

Anindita: Bye Jack.

I also retired to bed with a book, which I had purchased the other day. It was a tension-free night. I enjoyed reading till midnight and sometimes thought how I had got involved with financial activities, which I had never thought of! However, my dream of purchasing a flat for free living of poor meritorious girls who will come to the city for study purpose will be materialized if I get the fund from RBI, so I was dreaming of good things I would do in the future. I was a weird person no doubt. I kept on thinking how I should utilize my time and a portion of my savings for the benefit of poor but meritorious girl children of our society through my NGO. My friends appreciated my work but no one comes forward with financial help or with any other contribution. So I was really grateful to Jack for his good gesture, but it was under the scanner of government rules and regulations.

However, I had no other option but to wait and see when all formalities would be over and RBI would be kind enough to release the fund.

Saturday night when I logged to chat window, Mark Bright pinned me first.

Mark: Hi sweetheart, how are you?

Anindita: Mark where did you disappear for so many days? You were supposed to discuss your travel plan with me. You did not show up in given time. I felt insulted.

Mark: Oh no Anna. Please forgive me. I had to go to Liverpool on urgent business.

Anindita: Liverpool! Why? What is so special about Liverpool?

Mark: I shall tell you later. But now I am almost done with my plans and projects related to my visit to India.

Anindita: Really? I did not want to know your plans but I am very much doubtful how would you manage it alone in India!

Mark: You will be there, won't you?

Anindita: Don't be silly. I will not be any help for your business.

Mark: Ok sweetheart, you need not worry. I know how to proceed about my project. You please give me your cell number, I shall give you a call as soon as I reach Mumbai Airport. It will be early in the morning on 28th May.

Anindita: OMG! You are crazy, why do you want to move so fast?

Mark: You know Anna, I have purchased three different bottles of perfume for you. Hope you will love it.

Anindita: Mark how do you know that I shall accept it from you?

Mark: You are my friend, why should you not accept it?

Anindita: We Indian woman are very conservative, don't you know that? We don't accept things from stranger.

Mark: Hey, what is this? Am I a stranger to you after so many days friendship!

Anindita: Yes, this virtual friendship has no practical value, is it not?

Mark: No dear, I value our friendship, you are so dear and dependable, trustworthy, I really like you.

Anindita: Okay okay, I get it. You must be having a drink and that induces you to talk all such high-spirited words. It's getting late at night, I must go to sleep. Bye.

Mark: Bye dear, see you tomorrow at same time.

I expected that Jack would open chat but he did not. I was worried about his health. But I did not pin him as I knew he must be busy with his work. But I loved to reread our chatting of previous days, so whenever he was not there, I opened our previous conversations and read it again and again. It gave me immense pleasure as I could feel how much he was concerned about me. While I was reading it, Jack appeared.

Jack: Honey, are you there? I am sorry for being late.

Anindita: Okay it's alright. How are you?

Jack: Exhausted dear. Another problem is my net connectivity is almost finished, I doubt how long I could chat with you.

Anindita: Why? Don't you have unlimited connectivity?

Jack: No dear, I forgot to recharge it.

Anindita: But you could recharge it online also, I suppose.

Jack: No, I doubt it can be done right now. Anyway, how are you doing my angel?

Anindita: Ok. How is your health?

Jack: Not well at all. Doctor advised me to be hospitalized for thorough check-up but you know I can't do it right now.

Anindita: That's very bad, you should take care of your health first.

Jack: Yes honey, I know that but situation is not permitting me.

Anindita: Jack your new profile picture is lovely, but it must be an old picture of yours, actually I asked you to post a recent picture.

Jack: Dear, I did not get time to take it. Some other day I would appear, ok. My connectivity will get off now. Please excuse me. Just know I love you so much.

Anindita: What shall I do with your love, which causes only anxiety for me.

Jack: Honey, don't say so. You are my world. We shall meet soon and enjoy each other company, keep hope dear. Take care of yourself.

Anindita: Same to you. Bye.

Jack's Internet connection was off. So I closed chat. I was worried about him.

The next two days I kept myself busy by watching TV as tension was mounting high in our state for the Lok Sabha election. Kolkata went on polling on Monday 12th May, the last day of the polls. It was a holiday for us but not in other places. In Delhi it was a working day, so Reserve Bank could have released fund into my account, but they didn't. So I was anxious, and at once SMS to Mr John requesting him to find out what was happening at RBI. He replied me not to worry about it as he was keeping track. I knew that the man would not be able to do anything against the rules and regulations of RBI but at least he should tell me what else I had to do to get the fund, but it appeared that he did not know it.

Sunday night was uneventful as Jack did not appear for chatting, maybe he could not fix the Internet connection. Even Mark was not available. In fact, I did not have the mood for chatting also.

I Skyped with my son for some time and felt happy. After all there is nothing like a family. My son was very close to me till he completed his Higher Secondary, but he had grown up since and was busy with his study, project, presentation, etc. that sometimes he could not talk to me even over cell. I would get mad but this evening he gave me good news that he would be coming home by the end of May.

But my happiness was so transitory! I didn't want to share all the stress I had gone through during the past two weeks, as there was a bolt one after another from RBI demanding charges on different counts like Account Reflection charges and thereafter Account Up Gradation charges through E-mail, and I had no way but to comply with them hoping someday or the other they were going to release the fund. To my utter surprise, one Mr Richard called me from London and introduced himself as GM of Skypack Courier Service.

He wanted to assure me that if I pay Account Reflection charges and Account Upgrading charges there would be no other charge demand from RBI, as their company had signed a contract with RBI in this regard. I asked him to forward the contract to my E-mail but he said due to confidentiality it cannot be forwarded. However, again I had to remit fund to meet RBI demand. Mr John instructed me where to deposit money and I just followed his instructions and received E-receipt from RBI every time. My mind was not working anymore, as all my lifetime saving I had put in this high-risk transaction with the hope that at the end my expenditure will be squared off when RBI will release the fund.

My dear friend Jack also kept on assuring me that at first chance he will replenish my charges. And eventually he wrote to me that he was going to attend undersea project by 20th May, and as he would not be able to connect net from there, he would like to close his existing profile in FB to avoid any intruder access to his profile during his absence. I did not know what he meant by that but he gave me another profile address of his and asked me to send friend request for acceptance by him. I was surprised, and could not help it, but just did whatever he said.

I was so afraid of demurrage charges of RBI that I did not want a repetition of the same, so I had to move fast. It was difficult to accumulate money but it was not impossible. I kept on paying charges like "Signing of documents by RBI officials and Governor" and "Legalization of documents."

One night, Jack called me on cell and said,

"Honey, I could arrange INR fifty lakh to send you towards your expenses, hope you will be little relieved. I can't open chat due to some problem of my laptop. But please don't worry, I will be always there for you. Just know, I love you very much."

Anindita: Jack I don't understand why have you closed or blocked your FB account!

Jack: Dear, your son will be at home soon, you said. He should not look into our very personal chats so I thought it's better to close it for the time being.

Anindita: How ridiculous! Do you think my son will interfere in my personal matter. I can't believe that you have such a narrow outlook.

Jack: Honey, this new generation young people know to use the computer better than us, so I thought we should not be exposed.

Anindita: Shame on you. This is cowardliness do you realize it?

Jack: Honey, I will be under the sea for long time, so I thought...

Anindita: Anyway I could not appreciate your act. However, how did you send money this time?

Jack: Through UNO.

Anindita: Hope there will not be again any problem with that fund, no further charge will be asked for.

Jack: No honey, it is very much legal way to send money.

Anindita: Okay, I am so fed up with all the procedure, now I wish it would come to an end.

Jack: Yes honey, it will be ended to your satisfaction. Honey, just keep faith in me and know I love you so much.

Anindita: Okay all the best for your new undersea project work, do well. Bye.

Jack: Bye honey.

My happy and easy-going life had become so complicated due to Facebook friendship. I detested Facebook, and did not look at postings of my other friends even. However, I couldn't help but open private chat to see if Jack was there or Mark Bright. Both of them were not available nowadays. I was getting mad. The heat of the summer and happenings of my life, both were unbearable.

On 28th May morning at around ten o'clock, I received a call from Mark Bright.

Mark: Anna I am at Mumbai Airport, and having a problem.

Anindita: What problem?

Mark: I was carrying a box of cash GBP, Airport Customs confiscated it.

Anindita: What can I do about that?

Mark: Please listen to the Custom Officer, she wants to tell something to you. He handed over his cell phone to someone.

Custom Officer: Hello, Mr Bright landed at Mumbai Airport with huge cash, which is unlawful. He is telling us that he knows only you in India. Will you stand as guarantor for the money?

Anindita: Sorry, I did not get you. I hardly know Mr Bright, I can't be his guarantor in any case.

Custom Officer: So his money will be confiscated.

Anindita: Let it be, I can't help.

Mark: Anna, could you not help me in such situation? They are asking me to pay one lakh INR for Legalization certificate.

Anindita: Sorry, I can't help you. You better go back to London by return flight. I warned you earlier also not to come down to India without knowing rules and regulations well.

Mark: Anna, they will keep me in custody for how long, I don't know.

Anindita: It's your foolishness, I am sorry but really I am helpless.

I disconnected the call. As it is, I was so much deep in trouble for the RBI remittances, and Mark wanted to add another injury to my wound! I would go mad for sure!!

Next day, I received an E-mail from RBI as under:
Reserve Bank of India.
Reserve Bank of India
Central Office
RBI Regional Office 6, Sansad Marg,
New Delhi 110 001, India.
****

Dear Customer Anindita K
Date: 4th JUN 2014
Time: 1:30PM

WE WANT TO INFORM YOU CONCERNING THE FINAL STAGE OF YOUR TRANSACTION, AND WISHING YOU CONGRATULATIONS AS THE UNITED NATION HAS DEPOSITED FIFTY LAKH ON YOUR BEHALF AS COMPENSATION FOR EXPENSES YOU HAS MADE SO FAR ON THIS TRANSACTION AND WE WANT LET YOU KNOW

THAT YOUR MONEY WILL BE TRANSFERRED TO YOUR ACCOUNT TODAY.

SEQUEL TO THIS, WE REQUIRE YOU TO MAKE THE PAYMENT OF TEN LAKH SIX THOUSAND RUPEES FOR SECURITY DEPARTMENT OF RESERVE BANK OF INDIA WHO HAS BEEN MONITORING YOUR TRANSFER FOR SOME WEEKS NOW DUE TO ONLINE HACKERS AND THE TAX OF THE FIFTY LAKH, WHICH UNITED NATION HAS DEPOSITED ON YOUR BEHALF.

SO THE TOTAL AMOUNT YOU HAVE TO PAY BEFORE MONEY REFLECTS IN YOUR ACCOUNT TODAY IS TEN LAKH FOUR THOUSAND RUPEES, THE FINAL PAYMENT FROM THIS GREAT BANK. WE ARE SORRY FOR THE INCONVENIENCES WHICH WE MIGHT HAVE COST YOU.

We look forward to serving you better.

Best regards,

Mrs Sunita Anand
RBI.E-Banking/Online Wire Transfer Department.
Reserve Bank of India
Central Office
RBI Regional Office 6, Sansad Marg,
New Delhi 110 001, India.

Jack sent INR 50,00,000 to compensate my expenses but our forex regulator again made a claim on the amount! Why? Who will answer my queries? John was of no use. He was claiming back his money every other day without ensuring when I would get the fund. Though I had paid all the charges claimed by RBI, so far but they had again tagged the latest fifty lakh with the earlier one! They asked me to pay tax component and document signing charges from UN officials of INR ten lakh instantly so that they would release the entire INR of one crore eighty lakh. I had reached to the edge of my risk taking and fund raising ability, so I expressed my inability to pay further ten lakh to Mr John. He was sympathetic but told that if I did not pay, again all those demurrage charges may be applied, and asked me to try for the last time.

At night, I logged on to FB chat if Jack could be there. But in vain! He left a message for me, "Honey, I am very sick, hospitalized. Hope you will not have any problem with the UN fund and will get your entire dues very soon. Just know I love you so much."

On that calm but lonely midnight, tears poured down from my eyes just like incessant rain, I could not control myself. Why did I cry? Jack was sick, I could not interact with him and didn't know if he will ever call me. I missed him so much. He was supposed to start the undersea project this week, what will happen to that – all these thoughts kept me awake throughout the night. My own problem to arrange further ten lakh also appeared impossible to me. All my own sources were exhausted, how do I get the amount? I had no idea. The only option left was to intimate my husband and seek his help. I thought of doing so the next morning.

Next morning at 10.30 am, Mr John called me on my cell phone...

John: Madam, have you seen the latest E-mail from RBI?

Anindita: Yes I have seen. But Mr John why they have tagged UN fund with earlier remittance? I do not have any means to fulfill their demand. If they release earlier remittances, I could have paid the latest charge.

John: But madam, it is RBI Governor's instruction, how do we question that?

Anindita: I do not have any money left anywhere; their charges are in lakhs, not in thousands. A person like me does not have such huge means. I am totally broke. I find no way to arrange money. What do I do?

John: Madam, you should not retrieve now. Try hard.

Anindita: Mr John you try to borrow money on my behalf from the market. You are working in such a position in a reputed company, you can easily get loan, please try that for our mutual benefit.

John: Madam, I would love to help you but really I do not have any source. At the most, I will ask RBI official to accept the sum in installments and to give us some time for depositing the charges.

Anindita: But that will not solve the problem. At this stage I would not be able to raise ten lakh again.

John: Madam, why don't you understand. Any delay on your part again may attract demurrage charge.

Anindita: Mr John I am undone, not in a position to think what I should do.

John: Madam, RBI officials agreed with INR 5 lakh as first installment. Please arrange that as early as possible.

Anindita: Okay, if I can arrange I will call you.

Finally, I had to approach my husband for the money. He was very skeptical and did not believe the story of the remittances, but while I showed him the receipts of the various charges I had paid to RBI, with half-hearted trust he agreed to lend the money. He warned me that Nigerians are expert in making software and from their own remote domain operate through E-mail and loot money from various people. It was an important news story a few months back. He asked me to verify the remittance episode. I assured him about the genuine and high status of my Facebook friend. My husband hardly interfered in my activities, so he made no further queries but gave me a few deposit receipts for premature payment. I was relieved and went to bank, got the money, deposited to some odd accounts as Mr John asked me to do and received E-receipt from RBI. I was again waiting for release of entire sum.

Finally the D-day came and RBI asked me to log on RBI site http:/rbi-gov.in/login.php and I had to create user name and pin to update my bank account particulars.

I was asked to put that information secretly in an elaborate form. So for safety's sake, I filled in information from my own laptop.

And finally, they asked me to put on various codes like COT CODE, Tax Code, IMF Code, Demurrage Code, etc. on various fields.

I did not have any of those so-called codes so asked Mr John, to find out how to get those codes.

He said, "Madam, RBI will provide those codes one after another through E-mail and you will find money is being transferred to your account. You just follow their instruction meticulously." I was surprised to learn that after so many formalities and charges taken by RBI, I had to fill up codes, etc. myself, and if I made any mistake, the whole thing may be stuck up. I felt nervous and was waiting to get the codes. It was Friday afternoon and RBI mailed me COT Code. I put the code and saw money was being transferred and all thousand rupee notes were coming one after another and were transferred to my account. But only 25% of the transfer was made and it asked for the next code, which I have not received yet. Time was over, so I had to wait again till Monday, i.e., the next working day. I was a little apprehensive about the transfer procedure but what else could I do but to follow their instructions. I showed it to my husband and he asked me to consult one RBI auditor whom he knew, just to verify if things were moving in the right direction. He called him and narrated the entire episode. And the auditor told us that the site was a fake one. As per his knowledge, there was no such department at RBI New Delhi. I did not believe him and forwarded one of the mail and receipts from my E-mail to him just to ensure all those were genuine transactions. But he told me that all were fake; RBI did not have such a system. He told me that I had been robbed by cybercriminals and all my money was gone forever. But he advised me to lodge a complaint with Cybercrime Police Station at Lal Bazar, Kolkata who are authorized to handle such crimes. My head was reeling. I didn't know what to do. I fainted.

PART TWO

Cybercrime Police Station – Lal Bazar Kolkata

I was sitting at Cybercrime Police Station, Lal Bazar since 9 o'clock, waiting for the arrival of the officer-in-charge. The office was supposed to be open for 24 hours. One person was manning the office and he attended to me warmly and asked me what my problem was. I narrated to him my story in brief and he said, "After many months again this RBI remittance story is being reported. How much money did you lose?"

"I have not counted the total sum, but quite a few lakhs," I replied.

"From where did you get the money?" he questioned further.

"I am working, but presently am on sabbatical, my entire savings have gone," I explained.

"Madam, I am sorry to say that you will never get back your money," he stated."I have all the documents as to where I had sent the money, is not there any system to catch hold those culprits?" I asked, wanting to know what could be done.

"Madam, please wait in the lounge, the officer-in-charge will call you soon. He will guide you properly," he merely replied.

I realized that the person I was talking to may be a petty staff, but being in the department even he had acquired first-hand knowledge about cybercrime. I had no option but to wait for the OC to come. The police station was quite new and there was good arrangement for seating of the visitors, with cool AC room. So, with all my anxiety, I was sitting there with a blank head as I still did not believe that I have been cheated by my beloved Facebook friend Jack Smith. Mr John had called me even yesterday and asked me why I had not proceeded further and deposited the last leg of money to get the final code. I told him that I couldn't arrange money and so could not do that. He was very angry with me and asked me to send money in the first hour of Monday so that the process could be completed then and there and I would get my money. I was so perplexed and was about to shout at him and to tell that he was a cheat but somehow I controlled myself just to get some time to be sure about his modus operandi. I still had faith on Jack. He couldn't be a fraud for sure; he was not a fraudulent person, I was telling myself repeatedly.

At 11.30 am, the officer-in-charge came and asked me what has happened and after listening to me carefully, he asked me to submit a written application with all evidential documents so that they could start the investigation. He offered me a cup of tea even and was very sympathetic. But looking at the copies of RBI E-mails I took along with me, he also told me that all were fake and most probably a gang of Nigerian criminals were behind this operations. He told that they are expert in making software and cheating innocent rich people in different ways, and in a very few cases were the police able to catch hold of them.

I told him that those people will call me again on Monday for the last leg of money and asked, "Is it not possible to trap them at that point?"

He said that unless I lodged a written complaint they couldn't proceed.

Yes, he was right. My verbal compliant had no use, so I have to lodge a formal complaint first. I don't know how I did return home that day, I was not myself. It was such a shameful act on my part. I had lost all my credibility to my family. I could not expect any help from my husband. He warned me about the Nigerian scam, but I did not listen to him as I had faith on Jack's stature and his love for me. How would I tell my son about the whole affair! I didn't know what to do.

Monday morning

On Monday at around 11.30 am, John called me and asked when I was going to deposit the last leg of money. I could not control myself and shouted at him, how he dare to call me again after being a cheat all through! I disconnect his call, and to my utter surprise, Jack called me and asked what had happened? He said, "Honey, if you don't deposit the last leg I will lose my job, do you want that?"

I was stunned! How shameless, ruthless creatures these people were! Was there not any way to catch hold of them? There must be, I thought. But the hard reality was unveiled before me when I went to Lal Bazar again, a week later , for submitting my complaint.

It took me almost a week to arrange papers to write the complaint with all supporting documents. So far I had kept all these incidences within my family but my husband advised me to take the help of my relative who held a high position in the police department, as his reference might carry some weight.

So I called him and on hearing my story he was shocked and asked me why I did not refer to him before. I knew I was a fool not to verify it from RBI, but it never occurred to me to refer it to any police officer because I had faith on Jack and his love for me, I did not have any knowledge about cybercriminals, and their modus operandi. I trusted him so much. However, I didn't want to share my innermost feeling to others, so I could not respond to his queries. However, he was kind enough to accompany me to Lal Bazar Police Station, Detective Department, to lodge a formal complaint and introduced me to the officer-in-charge there.

Complaint at Lal Bazar Detective Department

I did not expect a warm welcome, but the officer-in-charge was very cordial and listened to my story carefully. He was sorry that this has happened to an educated, well-placed woman like me! Our conversation was as under:

Officer-in-charge: It's a clear case of Nigerian scam.

Anindita: What do you mean by that Sir? I do not understand.

Officer-in-charge: Don't you read newspapers?

Anindita: Yes I do, but there is hardly any good news nowadays. I skip bad news.

Officer-in-charge: Then how could you be aware of such a scam! Only few months back a detailed report was published in all leading newspapers regarding the Nigerian scam.

Anindita: It may have escaped my notice.

Officer-in-charge: That is most unfortunate; moreover, you have come to us after everything is over. There is hardly any room for us to take action in your case?

Anindita: Sir, I visited the Cybercrime Police Station a week before when those criminals were in action but nobody advised me the possibilities of tapping them but they have asked me to lodge formal complaint.

Sir, those culprits have sent me E-mails, SMS, even called me over telephone many a times. Is not there any possibility to detect their IP address, or the server from where they made this operation or service provider of the mobile must have their identity like, photo, home address, etc., from which police could trace those culprits.

Officer-in-charge: It's not that easy madam. You have approached us very late. By this time they have got enough time to wind up their trace from all those places. Another woman came to us when culprits were negotiating with her for money, and we were able to trace culprits by tracking their mobile conversations.

Anindita: Sir, I am totally broke, all my lifetime savings are gone. My NGO activities will come to an end. I don't know how I will live the rest of my life.

Officer-in-charge: I am sorry, but better forget your money. The culprits operate on commission basis. They tap local poor people with the pretention to help them in business by offering money to open a bank account with quite a few thousand and initially allowing them to operate the account. Then after some time, they take away signed cheque books and ATM cards from the account holders so that they can withdraw money from those accounts when people like you fall prey into their scheme.

Anindita: Sir, I have deposited money in reputed private sector bank's account holder, like ICICI Bank and Axis Bank, they must have taken proper KYC of their customers as per RBI guidelines and they must have CCTV footage at ATM or bank premises from where it is traceable as to who had withdrawn money from those accounts where I had deposited money as per the instruction of the agent, named John.

Officer-in-charge: You know so many things but did not know the scam! For such a long time you have helped them to cheat you but you never verified if things are genuine from RBI? You are an educated woman working in a responsible position, I wonder how you can be so ignorant.

Anindita: Sir, I did not doubt the status of my Facebook friend, he was supposed to be a graduate from London School of Economics, which was his USP to me. I was impressed with our chats. On various subjects we used to talk, he appeared to be quite knowledgeable; it never occurred to me that he could be a fraud.

Officer-in-charge: That is most unfortunate part of your story. You know, those criminals belong to such low grade in their society that you would not feel like talking to them even.

Anindita: Sir, Jack used to call me from his London number so often it never occurred to me that he may be a fraud.

Officer-in-charge: I doubt if he at all called from London. How was his accent? Like British?

Anindita: Not exactly like British but foreign accent.

Officer-in-charge: We Indians have this problem, anything foreign we just get carried away. He may have called you from India itself.

Anindita: No Sir, I have mentioned his London number in my application, you may verify that.

Officer-in-charge: Okay just see how I could also call you from that number sitting here in front of you.

He called me from that London number sitting before me. I did not know how it was possible. It must be a wonder of information technology. I was spellbound.

Officer-in-charge: This is the curse of technology. They are experts at it and are befooling us in so many ways. You know there was a businessman who was trapped like you and deposited lakhs of rupees in his friend's account as business deal but nothing came, no consignment he received from his partner. Finally, he came to us and we had nothing to do but to console him for his loss. He reported to us very late like you and we could not trace the culprits, but he did not believe us, and flied to London in search of his friend.

Anindita: Sir, did he find his partner in London?

Officer-in-charge: No, Scotland Yard could not help, finally he become a mental patient.

Anindita: Sir, don't tell me that you would not be able to do anything in my case.

Officer-in-charge: Yes, I am sorry but that is hard reality. They must have winded up their operation by paying commissions to the account holders and would have taken away the lion's share to their country.

Have you Skyped your friend?

Anindita: No Sir, once I asked him to log in Skype, but he told his net service is poor, it would not connect to Skype.

Officer-in-charge: That is another common pretext of cybercriminals. They never Skype with the plea that net connectivity is bad. All these symptoms confirm my doubt that it's a Nigerian scam.

Anindita: I can't believe this. Even if I don't get back my money, Sir, would you try to catch hold of those culprits?

Officer-in-charge: Yes, we will try to locate them, but in vain!

Anindita: Sir, why you are telling so?

Officer-in-charge: They are foreigners and are subject to International Laws. As per present Cybercrime Law 2008, maximum three years imprisonment they may get if they are proved to be guilty.

These criminals are very tech savvy and expert. They are trained in human psychology and advanced technology. They start their operation during summer and earn their fortune by cheating Indians and Asians mainly. Nigerians and Russians are expert in these lines. We are governed by the IT Act of 2000 and subsequent amendments during 2008, but those are not sufficient that much I can tell you.

Anindita: Sir, of all people, why did they target me?

Officer-in-charge: They may not have targeted you alone but hundreds other may have received the friend request from that person, but you turned lucky for him.

AninditaMadam, If you have any picture of your friend, show me. I will search our database in front of you in case he is one of our old clients!

I showed him a picture of Jack with his daughter, which I had saved in my mobile.

"Sorry, he is not in our record. But in most of the cases those criminals do not use their actual picture in their profile," the officer-in-charge replied.

I was listening to the officer and trying to relate things but could not actually believe what he had said. Somehow I still wanted to believe that Jack was not involved in the scam. He was such a nice friend and chatting with him was a pleasure for me.

However, I had to submit my complaint and the officer told me that if required, the department will call me sometime for further details, and proceeding will be started once it is allotted to an officer.

Enigma of life

A year had elapsed. Nothing had happened to my case. Cybercrime Police Station called me once to submit all my deposit receipts, which were to be a part of my complaint and would be deposited to the Criminal Court along with my application. For visiting the office of the Cybercrime Police Station, I had to collect a pass from the entry gate of Lal Bazar and every time the desk clerk used to ask if it were a case originated through Facebook! I used to be embarrassed, and tried not to answer as I could realize from the tone of the question that cheating through Facebook was a very common story. And they received many complaints on it.

The initial few months I hoped against hope to get any news from Cybercrime Police Station, but in vain! I dare not question the OC how far they had proceeded, what was their mode of enquiry. I knew that it was my fault. I realized even Mark Bright was a fraud, he wanted to cheat me in a different way but was not successful as by that time all my means were exhausted and I was not interested in his venture.

Surprisingly, since then, there has been a flow of E-mails in my mailbox in the name of different companies, like COCA COLA, BMW Car, Reader Digest, even in the name of RBI informing about receipt of this and that lucky draws, million dollar lotteries, etc. Now I know that these are called spam mails, which one should never believe and open but should delete from mailbox immediately.

Since then I have read all news on cybercrime, in newspapers. Now I read them with intense care and find how many ways cybercriminals operate to cheat people. Sometimes government also publishes notifications on cybercrime to alert the public. But in our country, how many people read the newspaper? What has happened to me would not have happened if I have read the stories that appeared in newspaper earlier.

I was surprised to note their various modus operandi. Even one Bollywood actor cum producer was victim of cybercrime and was cheated by his Facebook friend by few lakhs of rupees with the pretext of investment for producing a film jointly.

Other day, I was watching afternoon news in 24 hours News Channel, and suddenly one news flash drew my attention. It was about a cybercrime. One young man from a village of South Bengal was narrating how he was cheated through cable TV. He told that one day he was watching TV where a quiz contest was going on and the anchor introduced himself as TATA Motors' representative and asked to answer a simple question, which was to be replied through SMS. The young man replied correctly and received a congratulatory message in his mobile. It was stated that he owned a Tata Motor car as prize and it would be delivered to his address shortly. The whole family was excited and waited for the car to be delivered. But as usual, they were asked to deposit registration fees of the car, thereafter road tax, delivery charges, etc., one after another upfront. The poor family did not have means to fulfill those demands and they tried to collect money by pledging their house. Only then, they came to know that it was a cheating case. Cybercriminals used private cable channels also to cheat people.

It is very alarming that even poor villagers are being targeted by those criminals. How many cases our police could solve I have no idea. But I thought that if I write down my story it may create some awareness and someone may be saved.

After this incidence, my attitude towards life should have been changed but again I am a stupid woman who would never gave up or surrender to destiny. May be I am no longer wealthy but my philosophy of life, my education, my dream to extend a helping hand to poor girls will be there. My NGO was in the name of my late parents. Where ever they are they must be feeling very sorry for the suffering of their stupid girl but with their blessings I am fighting with the odds and I believe that someday or other I will regain strength to make my dream come true.

Annexure

A few samples of spam E-mails offering huge fortune to tap people

Tel: +447937426817

Dear Lucky Winner,

This is to inform you that your E-mail has won £750,000.00 (Seven Hundred and Fifty Thousand Great British Pounds) from the BMW Company United Kingdom, which is organized by World Bank and UK Mobile Company in conjunction with Chevron Texaco Oil and Gas Company. "Your E-mail address" was selected through a computer ballot system drawn from Nine hundred thousand E-mails from Canada, Australia, United States, Asia, Europe, Middle East, Africa and Ocean Pacific as part of our international program, which is conducted annually. 20 people were selected as our winners, through electronic ballot system without the winner applying.

FILL THIS FORM FOR PRIZE RELEASE:-

1 Full Name:

2 Country:

3 Address:

4 Phone Number:

5 Marital Status:

6 Occupation:

7 Sex :

8 Age:

These are your identification numbers:

Ticket Number: 011425896/2016

Serial Number: 3872/506

Lucky Numbers: 7/4/88/28/01/40

Make sure you send your detail to this E-mail (bmw.claimsdpt@tech-center.com) for the release of your fund.

Due to possible mix up of some numbers and E-mail contacts, we ask that you keep this winning strictly from public notice until your claim has been processed and your money is being remitted to you. This is part of our security protocol to avoid double claims or unscrupulous acts by some participants of this program. Please do not reply if you are not the owner of this E-mail address.

Yours Faithfully

CHEVROLET AUTOMOBILE COMPANY

Chevrolet UK PLC, Griffin House,

UK1-101-135, Osborne Road,

Luton, Bedfordshire LU1 3YT

Register company number: 4533384

chevroletcardraw@hotmail.com

Telephone:+448712348592

STAR PRIZE WINNER

This is to inform you that you have won a BRAND NEW Chevrolet Cruze 2013 MODEL CAR and cash prize of (350,000GBP). The car comes with a special CHEVROLET INSURANCE Cover for one whole year till the next promotion. It also comes with a one-year warranty and FREE repairs at any CHEVROLET AUTOMOBILE depot or service center worldwide. Your Batch No: 515944052/166 and Winning No: 1544 make you as one of the lucky winner in our 2014 Charity bonanza. You are to contact our claims manager on this E-mail: chevroletcardraw@hotmail.com with the below details for claims. Please Fill the Information below: A scan copy of your identification (Driving License or any Valid ID Proof) is needed.

1. Full Name:
2. Full Address:
3. State:
4. Occupation:
5. Age:
6. Sex:
7. Country:
8. Winning E-mail:
9. Mobile Number:
10. Banking Details:
11. Account Name:
12. Account Number
13. Bank Name And Branch

10. Ensure that you send all your information to chevroletcardraw@hotmail.com to enable us responds back immediately.

NOTE:- YOU ARE TO IMMEDIATELY SEND YOUR COMPLETE INFORMATION FOR CLAIMS ON THIS E-MAIL ONLY:- chevroletukunite1@hotmail.com

भारतीय रिज़र्व बैंक
Reserve Bank of India

THE RESERVE BANK OF INDIA
ELECTRONIC TRANSFER DEPT. 6, SANSAD MARG
JANPATH, NEW DELHI, H.O. 110001,
NEW DELHI

Our ref: Cub/Hog/Oxd1/2012
Payment file: RBI/id1033/201/2015. Reply To RBI Email: rbionlinetransfer41@outlook.com
Payment amount: 4.CRORE, 98.LAKHS = 500,000 GBPS

RESERVE BANK OF INDIA OFFICIAL COMPENSATION PAYMENT NOTIFICATION

Dear Beneficiary:

The Foreign Exchange Transfer Department (RBI) hereby bring to your attention of the payment of your deposited fund here in the RBI, you were listed as a beneficiary in the recent schedule for payment of the past edition email/sms award incurred by the BRITISH GOVERNMENT, which is yet unclaimed up-till date due to some circumstance.

According to your file record; your payment is categorized as: Contract type: Lottery/inheritance/Undelivered Lottery fund/

The Reserve Bank of India (RBI) Governor, Dr Raghuram Rajan and Ban Kin-moon Secretary-General of the United Nations met with the Tax Committee on Finance RBI Mumbai/Delhi branch. Regarding unclaimed funds which have been due for a long run, At the end of the meeting (RBI) Governor, Dr Raghuram Rajan mandate all unclaimed funds to be released back to the beneficiary stating that it is an unfair practice to withhold funds for government basket for one reason or the other for tax accumulations. Therefore, we are writing this email to inform you that *(4CROER 98LAKHS INDIA RUPEES)* **will be release to you in committed for (RBI) Governor that Beneficiary will have to pay crediting fees only. In cash deposit. To credit your account immediately making a decline for 2 working days after date of receiving this mail Also reconfirm your details- for crediting (RBI) Governor.**

To credit your account immediately you will have to send copy of your Pan/Voter card, and one picture of your passport size for file record, This is according to law assigned
Also reconfirm your details- for crediting. Please you are advised to fill the form below and send it immediately to our transfer department through email below for verification and prompt collection. Contact transfer Manager in charges of foreign exchange Transfer department Contact Person: Mrs Sonia Sharma

FILL THE VERIFICATION FORM BELOW FOR PROMPT COLLECTION OF YOUR FUND.

1. Full Names:
2. Residential Address:
3. Mobile Number:
4. Occupation:
5. Sex:
6. Age:
7. Country:
8. Marital Status:
9. Passport Size Photo: / Scan Copy ID Proof
10. E-mail id:
11. Bank Name:
12. A/c No:
13. A/c Holders Name:
14. Bank Branch:
15. Bank Swift or Ifsc code;

Reply to Reserved Bank of India Email Id: (rbionlinetransfer41@outlook.com)

NOTE (4CROER 98LAKHS INDIA RUPEES) ***will be transfer directly to your Bank Account immediately we receive your filled details. Also be informed that the assigned British representative to supervise the transfer of your fund from the Reserve Bank is in the person of: (BRITISHDIPLOMAT) MR JOHN LARRY. He will supervise the transfer and all the documents will be sent to you by courier immediately the transfer of your fund is complete to you.***

For more details visit the link below: http://www.financialexpress.com/news/find-whereabouts-of-unclaimed-deposit-holders-rbi-tells-banks/909041